THE HOME FRONT

THE HOME FRONT
The British and the Second World War

ARTHUR MARWICK

Photographic research by Harold Chapman

with 167 illustrations

THAMES AND HUDSON · LONDON

Frontispiece: families sheltering
in a tunnel during the
Battle of Britain, 1940.

*Filmset and printed in Great Britain
by BAS Printers Limited, Wallop, Hampshire*

Contents

Preface

Historical research has become such a joy since my early post-graduate days, when some librarians at least seemed more concerned to preserve rather than share information. I should like to acknowledge with deep gratitude the enormous help which I have received from all the archivists and librarians at the various archives which are listed below. Above all I should like to thank Roderick Suddaby and Elizabeth Hook and their colleagues at the Imperial War Museum, who always ensured that my visits there were not only pleasant, but extremely rewarding.

My debt to Harold Chapman, picture researcher and professional photographer, is more fully explained in Chapter One. From him I have learned a great deal about the nature of photographic evidence. On this score I should also like to express my thanks to John Topham, to Alan Smith of Popperfoto, to Bert Garri of the Keystone Press Agency and to Mike McEwan of the *Daily Express*

Margaret Keech typed the first draft of this book, and Peggy Mackay prepared the final version: my best thanks go to both of them.

Among the more traditional sources, apart from government publications, social surveys and newspapers, I have made most use of the following: the twenty or so collections of private letters and diaries now housed in the Department of Documents at the Imperial War Museum; the BBC Written Archives at Caversham Park; the Beveridge Papers and the Dalton Diaries in the British Library of Political and Economical Science (together with less directly relevant collections); the Attlee Papers, divided between University College, Oxford, and Churchill College, Cambridge; the Bevin Papers, the Margesson Papers and a number of other collections at Churchill College, Cambridge; the Monckton Papers and the Crookshank Diaries in the Bodleian Library, Oxford; the Cabinet and associated papers in the Public Record Office in Portugal Street, and the files of the various departments concerned with domestic and social affairs housed in the Public Record Office depository at Ashridge; papers in the Labour Party Library at Transport House and in the Conservative Research Department; the Liddell Hart Papers at Medmenham, Bucks; and the files of Mass Observation housed at the University of Sussex.

Like any source, the Mass Observation Files have to be treated critically and balanced against other evidence. Nonetheless, this independent non-profit making organization founded by Tom Harrisson and Professor Charles Madge, employing a team of full-time observers, together with a national panel of part-timers, who tried to maintain scientific standards in their observations and interviews, makes available uniquely valuable material for the study of the social history of the Second World War. Mass Observation provided evidence for many government and private bodies and published many important reports. But the files themselves have the special value that they were not intended for publication; indeed, when Captain Liddell Hart, in 1940, requested access to the Mass Observation file on refugees, Tom Harrisson, as the Liddell Hart Papers reveal, had to reply that 'official circles' would not permit this. I owe a very special debt to Tom Harrisson, whose sad death was announced just as this book was going to press.

For permission to consult and/or quote copyright texts, acknowledgments are due to: The Controller of Her Majesty's Stationery Office for Crown Copyright material; the late Tom Harrisson and the Mass Observation Archives at the University of Sussex; The Director and Trustees of the Imperial War Museum (H. E. Strong and Evans Papers); The Library of Congress (Laski-Huebsch correspondence); The British Library of Political and Economic Science (Beveridge Papers); The Centre for Military Archives, King's College, London, and Lady Liddell Hart; Mrs D. Brinton-Lee; Mr W. H. Haslam; Mr A. Mackay; Mrs F. Spragg (H. A. Penny Diary); Capt. A. V. S. Yates; Mr N. F. Ellison; Mr E. L. Mann; Mrs C. B. Smith (the late J. P. McHutchison); Mrs J. Reid (Miss Hilda Neal's Diary); Mrs K. M. Harding (née Kate Phipps); Mr G. H. P. Buchanan (Viscount Margesson Papers); Messrs Allen and Overy and the Trustees of the late Viscount Monckton of Brenchley.

CHAPTER ONE

Introduction: Sources and Controversies

I have tried to write this book almost as I would a film or television script, giving the photographs serious attention as valid historical sources, and endeavouring to weave my narrative round them. But since photographic evidence is only useful for certain things, my basic outline and analysis of events, as well as my classification of and commentary on the photographs, are inevitably based on the written and printed sources which are now available in profusion.

Naturally, I have worked very closely indeed with the picture researcher, Harold Chapman, who has marvellously combined a dedicated pursuit of my guidelines, with indefatigable research in the most intractable archives. It happens that many of the collections used are now owned by that excellent and ambitious agency Popperfoto: this should not be allowed to obscure the pioneer work which Harold Chapman did in basements and attics, sorting through uncatalogued material for which often only negatives existed. In this book, I have tried wherever possible to give the date, origins and original use of each photograph, and to indicate whether or not it was passed by the censor. Where I have been forced to limit myself to the (often unsatisfactory) caption recorded in the photographic archives, I have added quotation marks.

Photographs are silent witnesses, but very far from unbiased ones; they show only what cameramen chose, or were asked, to record, frequently with a good deal of conscious setting up and composition in advance. In wartime, conditions were particularly difficult for all communicators. In those days, when newspapermen still used heavy box-cameras and slides, pictures had to be taken carefully. Photographers for such important picture papers as *Illustrated* and *Picture Post* sometimes used film stock – but in wartime that was in very short supply. No cameraman was in any position to take a long series of rapid snaps.

Newspapers and photographers ran the risk of heavy penalties if they published anything of which the authorities disapproved. In practice, all photographs which touched on a subject remotely sensitive in regard to the war effort were submitted in advance to the Censorship Bureau. Many of the photographs which I have used in this book were stamped 'Not passed by Censor'. Nevertheless, in the atmosphere of wartime, censorship was perhaps less vexatious than might be thought. Most newspaper editors, most journalists and most cameramen shared the same assumptions about the national interest as did the Government. By and large there was a strong desire to create the kind of morale-boosting pictures which have become part of the mythology of the war, and a wish to avoid taking anything which might be embarrassing to the national effort.

Resources were pooled during the war, and many of the best-known pictures were simply agency photographs. However, John Topham had already singled himself out before the war as an independent photographer of great originality and flair. This book contains a number of Topham photographs which do sometimes help to penetrate behind the rather formalized official view of the Home Front.

Apart from traditional written sources, I have made great use of the newsreels, feature films and documentaries of the Second World War. As appropriate, I have made some references to these sources in the course of this book. But the visual material reproduced has been confined exclusively to photographs, excluding, for example, paintings and cartoons, in themselves well worth separate study. Recently, Susan Briggs in *Keep Smiling Through* (1975) has shown how the popular songs of the period can be linked up with the visual material: I have not sought to compete with her.

Much of what is written or said about the Home Front in the Second World War is myth rather than history. This is perfectly understandable. The war was a very powerful experience for those who lived through it. At the time, all the resources of the mass media and of national propaganda were mobilized in the direction of presenting certain aspects of the war and suppressing others. Looking back, people tend to remember what they want to remember, and to suppress the less pleasant parts of the war experience. Our politicians have not been backward in invoking the glories of the war in an attempt to take us through the economic difficulties of the present. Broadly speaking, the notions evoked by the Home Front tend to be along the lines of: 'national unity and mixing of social classes', 'heroism and humour in face of the dangers of the Blitz', and 'hard work and grim determination producing victory against powerful odds'.

More recently, historians have begun to look critically at some of the popular assumptions about the nature of the Second World War. While taking over the cliché phrase 'The People's War' for his brilliant large-scale survey of British society in the Second World War, Angus Calder made use of it in a deeply ironical way. People worked and fought bravely, but they were often discontented, and in the end they were conned: 'The effect of the war was not to sweep society on to a new course,' Dr Calder argued, 'but to hasten its progress along the old grooves.' Calder's sceptical views were seconded by one of the most respected of all scholars working in the field of twentieth-century British history, Henry Pelling, among other things the first full biographer of Winston Churchill. Only one short chapter in his short book, *Britain and the Second World War*, was devoted to the Home Front and questions of social change, but Dr Pelling was clear and forceful in his view that the war had had no very profound effect on British society. This side of the argument was further reinforced by Tom Harrisson who, as founder of Mass Observation and a distinguished anthropologist and historian in his own right, has every claim on our attention. On television and in the press (and no doubt in his forthcoming book on aerial bombing, which had not appeared at the time this was being written) Tom Harrisson lambasted the myths about national unity and heroism in the Blitz, pointing out the snobbish nature of the establishment, the inadequacy of the provision that they made for air-raids, and the not unnatural reactions of dismay and even despair aroused among those who suffered the brunt of the bomb-attacks.

There is usually more basic agreement between historians and authors than sometimes appears on the surface; but it could be broadly said that I (particularly in my books *Britain in the Century of Total War* and *War and Social Change in the Twentieth Century*) have tended to be identified with a slightly different approach from that of Calder, Pelling and Harrisson. I believe that there is some truth in the myths, and that, above all, for good or ill, the Second World War did profoundly change British society. In part, of course, judgment depends upon what your standards are, what sort of change you believe to be possible in human society. It is no reflection on Angus Calder's impeccable scholarship to point out that he is a committed socialist. Without any doubt at all, the Second World War did not produce a socialist society. But I would prefer to take as my standard of measurement the state of British society in the 1930s, rather than some hypothetical ideal state: by this standard, I argue, British society did change, even if not nearly as much, or in the directions, that some would wish. Most recently this approach, stressing the changes that actually did take place without any attempt to exaggerate the development towards a classless society or socialist democracy, has been developed in a book which fully merits the rave reviews which it has received – Paul Addison's *The Road to 1945: British Politics and the Second World War* (1975).

There is no such thing in historical writing as leaving the evidence to speak for itself. At best, such an approach results in a collection of sources, not a complete history. I hope the reader will find the photographs, and the various extracts from written documents which I have included, as worthy of some attention in their own right. But inevitably this book will follow a line which approaches nearer to Addison than to Calder. At the same time, I hope I have taken due cognizance of the very salutary correctives to popular mythology administered by Calder, Pelling and Tom Harrisson. There are few final answers in historical study: much depends on the questions you ask, and almost as much on the method you adopt in approaching the sources. In previous books I have attempted to resolve some of the problems of war's impact on society by breaking war down into four 'dimensions': war as 'destruction and disruption'; war as a 'test' of existing institutions; war as involving the 'participation' of hitherto under-privileged social classes and groups; and war as a great 'psychological experience'. This kind of analysis I shall leave for only the very briefest treatment at the end of the book, in the hope that for the rest, even if evidence cannot speak for itself, it can be enjoyed without undue outside interference. The main structuring I have done is chronological: the war, after all, was not over in one blinding instant – attitudes and reactions developed slowly across a period of six years.

The first phase, from shortly before the war (I have included a section on 'the pre-war scene' and have touched on the Munich crisis, which, at the time, seemed likely to precipitate war in September 1938) to the Battle of Britain in the summer of 1940, I have termed 'From Illusions to Reality'. 'Illusions' perhaps is a strong word. But certainly British attitudes in the early stages of the war were governed by what people imagined the war was going to be like, rather than by the war as it actually turned out. If not imaginary, the war in the period of the conquest of Poland and its aftermath was pretty invisible to the British public, and did not seriously or directly impinge on British society till the early summer of 1940. With Dunkirk followed rapidly by the Battle of Britain, and then by the Blitz, it suddenly became realistically clear that the Home Front was also a kind of Front Line.

The next phase is that of 'the Blitz', from September 1940 to the late spring of 1941. Bomb-attacks by no means ceased then, but the worst sustained period of what Lord Butler has described as 'the ritual existence and constant peril of the Blitz' was over. The phase of 'Austerity' I have defined as falling between 1941 and 1943, though in fact austerity continued until the end of the war and beyond. Here I have tried to pin down the quality of life in the often tedious middle period of the war.

There is evidence of something of a lifting of spirits and a new interest in the future in the period from the end of 1942 till the end of the war. I have termed this the phase of 'Social Change', though I have also noted the social deterioration which was the inevitable consequence of the destructiveness of war, as well as looking at some of the deeper changes which I believe to have taken place in regard to social welfare, the position of labour and the trade unions, the position of women and so on.

Then, since one of my purposes is to set the war in a wider perspective, I have short chapters on '1945 and After' and on the overall social consequences of the complete war experience.

CHAPTER TWO

From Illusions to Reality:
September 1939–September 1940

1 The Pre-War Scene

Among the papers of Captain David Margesson (created Viscount Margesson in 1942), Government Chief Whip at the outbreak of war, is an unpublished and unattributed typescript entitled 'Chamberlain: A Candid Portrait'; the document was obviously written just after the war started, and it may well have been the work of Margesson himself, since its final conclusion is that now that war has begun Chamberlain, as Prime Minister, will fight with determination. The document reads in part:

For two-and-a-half years, Neville Chamberlain has been Prime Minister of Great Britain. During this period Great Britain has suffered a series of diplomatic defeats and humiliations, culminating in the outbreak of European war. It is an unbroken record of failure in foreign policy, and there has been no outstanding success at home to offset the lack of it abroad. . . . Yet it is probable that Neville Chamberlain still retains the confidence of the majority of his fellow country-men and that, if it were possible to obtain an accurate test of the feelings of the electorate, Chamberlain would be found the most popular statesman in the land. These facts are remarkable, and require explanation. . . .

The truest explanation may be that they [his fellow country-men] see in him a reflection of themselves and that therefore they feel that he is one they can understand and can trust.

The English respect ability, but they distrust brilliance. For them the very word 'genius' carries with it something derogatory. It connotes unconventional clothes and doubtful morals. . . .

The ordinary Englishman sees in him an ordinary Englishman like himself; one who has been in business in a small way and has made a little – but not much – money; one who has been happily married and brought up a family of which the world knows little; one who wears the same business-suit everyday, the black coat and vest, the striped trousers, the laced boots, and carries the same umbrella whether he is walking on a cloudless morning in the Park with Mrs. Chamberlain (which he does everyday at the same hour) or whether he is flying across Europe to meet a dictator and settle the affairs of nations.[1]

Indeed, when Chamberlain averted war in September 1938 by giving way to Hitler's demands at Munich, he apparently had the support of the vast majority of the wealthy and respectable classes, those who thought like him and dressed like him. They joined in prayers for peace (*Plate 1*).

The professional and clerical classes were doing reasonably well in the 1930s. Mortgages were cheap, and the new suburbia was booming.

1 September 1938. Political crisis. People entering Westminster Abbey to pray for peace.

Opposite:
3 European crisis, 1938: evacuation. *News Chronicle* photograph of children of the Raphael Mackinnon School, Deptford, who had returned from the East Grinstead district.

Some members of the middle class could afford a modest car (*Plate 4*). Here in the suburbs, if anywhere, was to be found peacetime tranquillity and a sense of insulation from the anguish and protest of industrial Britain. Tranquillity and insulation – both were to be shattered by the bombs of wartime.

It is not surprising that people were relieved by the Munich settlement, or that they prayed for peace. If war came, it was expected (on the model of the Spanish Civil War) to be a devastating bombing war; and the terror which loomed large in everyone's minds was gas, rather than high explosives or incendiaries. Bomb-attacks would mean evacuating children and others from danger areas, and small-scale evacuations were in fact carried out at the height of the Munich crisis (*Plate 3*). The gas menace never materialized, but the threat exercised a powerful hold over the popular imagination (*Plate 2*).

Whatever support there might be for Chamberlain's Government in prosperous suburban areas, there was in fact bitter hostility to him in many other parts of the country. Britain in the thirties was a divided

2 Gas-proof pram, December 1938. The story, dated 8 December 1938 and filed by John Topham, read as follows. 'Mr. E. W. Mills, a nurseryman of Hextable, Kent, has invented a gas proof perambulator, made in his spare time. It has the approval of the local ARP [Air-Raid Precautions] committee. Picture shows a demonstration of a mother taking her child to an air-raid shelter during a raid – both protected from gas. The pram is constructed of wood, has a triplex glass window, an air valve, a filter from a gas mask (protected from wet weather by the cowling) and a large bulb at the rear to pump out the air. When the bulb is pressed air is forced out via the valve, and the air is let in via the filter.'

4 Rochester Way, south-east
London, 1939.

5 Lancashire hunger marchers: leaving Woodstock on the way to London via Oxford, 4 November 1936.

society. Unemployment still ran at over a million on the outbreak of war, and hunger marches from the depressed areas to the capital had been a recurrent feature (*Plate 5*).

Plate 5 merits very close attention, both as a general symbol of the condition of Britain in the thirties, and for the detailed information contained on the banner. One of the most characteristically ludicrous developments in social policy had been the attempt of the privately sponsored, but government supported, Land Settlement Association to provide land holdings for the unemployed. Training for their new careers in agriculture was given to the unemployed in camps, often run on militaristic lines. The tone of the whole operation, which not surprisingly was a complete fiasco, was patronizing in the extreme. Thus the banner demands work and wages, not 'slave camps' – a reference to the land settlement project.

Although the social services had been expanded during and after the First World War, they still contained many gaps. In general, they were confined to the working class, and, in many cases, were only available after an applicant had undergone a strict Means Test which took all possible family sources of income into account, not just those of the applicant himself. Medical provision was particularly inadequate. Only the insured worker himself, not his wife or his children, received free treatment, as a 'panel' patient. There was a pretty blatant class distinction between being a 'panel' patient and being a 'fee-paying' patient. The cold war waged in some areas between 'voluntary' hospitals and 'local authority' hospitals added to the inefficiencies and anomalies of health care. Many hospitals depended for survival on their flag days.

The received attitude towards medical provision is strongly brought out in the British Medical Association's statement on 'Hospital Policy' of June 1939, which was actually intended to be a programme of change. After remarking that hospitals had originally been designed only for the destitute poor, but that they now catered for the 'class above', that is 'the lower paid workers', the report continued:

The Association recognises that there is, in many areas, a shortage of institutional provision for the person belonging to the so-called middle class. Although his income is above that usually accepted for hospital purposes, with the result that he cannot properly be treated in the public ward of a voluntary hospital, it is often insufficient to cover the cost of a privately established Nursing Home. The Association welcomes the development of pay-beds in association with the hospitals at fees within the capacity of middle class patients.[2]

'It is undesirable', declared the document, capturing the essence of a whole social philosophy, 'that private patients should be seen or treated at the out-patient department of a hospital. . . .'

For those who could not afford to live in the suburbs or on the new local authority housing estates, housing conditions could be appalling. In 1938 a rent strike movement began in the East End of London. In many areas the ordinary working man, perhaps lacking confidence in

6 Langdale Mansions, Stepney, 28 June 1939. Families of rent strikers, evicted after the battle between strikers and police and bailiffs, defied the authorities by moving back in.

himself, was not always very good at standing up for his rights; but in Stepney a Tenants Defence League, presided over by Father Groser, an Anglo-Catholic priest, with 'Tubby' Rosen, a Communist, as secretary, was founded. Most landlords gave in, but the landlord of Langdale Mansions did not (*Plate 6*). Although the landlords made the hoary old appeal to 'law and order' against 'mob law', the tenants eventually won the concessions they were seeking. The words on the banner read 'Chamberlain must go' – the simple, potent, political slogan which expressed the great divide in British society on the outbreak of war and the hostility felt towards the Government which Chamberlain personalized.

British society had undergone many important developments since the previous war. Most of the egalitarian processes initiated by the war had continued, so that some of the worst class shibboleths of Edwardian and Victorian times had vanished for ever. But class distinctions were still much in evidence. Above all, the vast majority of the British people felt a deep sense of insecurity: the threat of war was not more immediate than the threat of unemployment and social deprivation.

Since February 1939 there had been a series of small incidents throughout the country involving explosives. On Friday 25 August 1939 five people were killed and many others injured when a bomb placed in the basket of a tradesman's bicycle blew up in Broadgate, Coventry. Responsibility lay with the IRA. There were a number of demonstrations of anti-Irish feeling. But, as in 1914, the lesser violence occasioned by the intractable problem of Ireland was swallowed up in the immensely greater violence created by that other intractable problem, Germany's relations with the rest of Europe.

2 War Breaks Out

Given the fears people had of bombs and gas, it can scarcely be said that the outbreak of war was welcomed: certainly there was none of the exuberance, none of the cheering of 4 August 1914. Then, in the heyday of monarchy and imperialism, the focal point had been Buckingham Palace. Now, since Chamberlain had made the policy of appeasement so very much a personal matter (his weary broadcast announcing the declaration of war, which has been used over and over again in war films, came near to presenting the war as a personal tragedy for himself rather than for Europe and the world), the focal point was the Prime Minister's residence in Downing Street. To point up the contrast, it may be noted that when at last the time came to celebrate victory, the crowds once more focused their attention on Buckingham Palace: there, the political leaders of a nation probably as nearly united as a nation is able to be – short of the unity of the grave – appeared together with the Royal Family.

7 The declaration of war: crowds in Downing Street on Sunday 3 September 1939.

At the outbreak of war, all the evidence suggests that the popular mood, insofar as one can talk of such a thing, was one of release from unbearable tension, of slightly fearful determination and of grim resignation. Three diary extracts, the first by a middle-class housewife, the second by a younger girl and the third by a man, give the authentic flavour:

It has happened! my first feeling was one of tremendous relief, that the awful waiting and uncertainty is over.

My friend, my sister and I, all under 30, agreed we would almost welcome the war. We turned on the radio, and hear Chamberlain's speech. I felt slightly sick, and yet half relieved.

The war has not had the effect of giving one broken night. After twelve months of broken sleep, when I knew the die was cast, my sleep returned.[3]

Another upper-middle-class lady was clear-eyed and ruthlessly honest with herself:

Now the thing was actually upon us, and I had had no heart to meet it. In 1914 we had had no idea of what we were in for, and we all I think felt excited, almost elated. There is not much glamour and excitement now for us about war. I feared that I was going to lose all the pleasures and activities, – the little *tatty* pleasures, as someone called them, that I found so dear, and I was sick at heart.[4]

In the First World War, conscription had not been introduced till 1916; but in 1939 both conscription and a national register of occupations were instituted a couple of days before the actual outbreak of war. But inevitably the first to be called up were the regulars and the

8 The first air-raid warning in London: people emerging from a shelter after the 'All Clear' had sounded, 3 September 1939.

9 Territorial leaves to join his regiment. This photograph, taken by John Topham on 3 September 1939, provides an intriguing example of how photographic evidence comes into being. Topham submitted it to the press sometime later with the following note: 'This picture was taken on Sidcup (Kent) station on the day that war broke out – 3rd. September, 1939, and shows the local parson saying his farewells to his son – a territorial in the Artists' Rifles.' Topham then continued: 'Would you like a follow-up feature of parson and son and if possible, the porter in the background?'

territorials. The intimacy and restraint of *Plate 9* is noteworthy, and can be contrasted with the enthusiasm of the group photographs of August 1914.

Within minutes of the declaration of war the air-raid sirens in London and the south-east went into operation, and people headed towards the public shelters which had been constructed in the last months of peace. On the whole it appears that people entered and left the shelters with that much-vaunted British calm (*Plate 8*): 'quite orderly and no hysterics' was a phrase used by a company director, some of whose friends had been caught in this first air-raid at Hammersmith in West London, in writing to his nephew in the Navy.[5] In fact the warning was a false alarm; there were several more, equally false, during the next days and weeks.

3 Evacuation (For Real?)

Well before the war, plans had been made for the evacuation of mothers and children from danger areas to reception areas, and, indeed, as we noted, a small-scale evacuation took place during the Munich crisis. The real evacuation, in rather muddled style, began on 1 September. The Government had planned to move about three-and-a half million people, but in the event rather less than one-and-a-half million made use of the official scheme. Almost all of them had reached the reception areas by the evening of 3 September, a few hours after the official declaration of war.

This was the wave of evacuation for which we have the most vivid pictures: whole groups of children, with labels round their necks, were sent together, with only a few mothers, teachers and members of the Women's Volunteer Service. Newsreels and newspapers presented evacuation as a rather exciting adventure, and there were plenty of obviously set-up pictures showing the children as happy, and the organization as impeccable. That was the public and official view; in the privacy of his own diary, a London bus driver, Henry Alexander Penny, was noting at the beginning of September with greater truth: 'It was a Pityful sight to see so many Thousands of small children, all labelled and carrying small cases and parcels. Some crying, some Happy, all going to strange Homes.'[6] Mel Calman (the cartoonist) recalls his own personal experience:

I have this image of a small boy with a label tied round his neck. The boy has no features and is crying. He is carrying a cardboard box, which contains his gasmask.

I remember that labels with our names on were pinned to our clothes before we left London. I think I felt that I had no identity and was a parcel being posted to the country. The labels frightened me as much as the idea of leaving my parents. A child of seven, if lost, can tell people his name. A label assumes that he does not know his name, or worse, has no name and is given one at random from a list of names.

10   Evacuation, 1939: children
reach their destination at
Eastbourne.

Perhaps the gasmask felt like a second face, a mask that would replace my own face as soon as I left London. I remember that the gasmask looked inhuman with its celluloid eyeshield and metal snout. I remember that it smelt of rubber and that I could not breathe properly inside it. The shield misted over with condensation and it felt warm and suffocating inside this second face.

I know that we rehearsed the evacuation every morning for a week. Each morning my sister and I would leave home with our packed sandwiches and clothes. We would say goodbye to our parents. Our labels were pinned on and I felt sick. We were not told the date of the real departure in case the Germans bombed the train. That seems hard to believe now, but at that time people seemed to find spies under their beds every night. So we had to leave home without knowing if we would return that day or not. We went through this awful ritual of goodbye every morning for a week. Every morning I felt sick and kissed my parents and felt I was leaving my name and identity with them.

Even nowadays whenever I travel anywhere and have to say goodbye to my own children, I identify with that small boy. I remember the label and the gasmask and feel anxiety gripping my bowels. I write my name on the luggage labels and hope I do not return to find my home bombed to ruins and my identity lost somewhere underneath the rubble.[7]

On the whole, it is the relatively small number of photographs of the children on arrival rather than departure which reveal the true pathos of evacuation (*Plates 10 and 11*). No photographs showed the rags in which some slum kids were clad, nor the lice and scabies which they brought with them.

In some areas reception arrangements were so haphazard that children were in effect auctioned off to whichever householders fancied whichever children.

11   Evacuation, 1939: children arriving at their billet. From the internal evidence of the photograph itself, this looks very like a case of lower-middle-class town children arriving at a lower-middle-class rural household. The man on the left is probably a school teacher responsible for securing billets for the children.

12 'See the Children', special
train: on arrival at Northampton
the parents were said to have
been greeted with cries of 'Oh!
Mum!'. *News Chronicle*
photograph, 4 December 1939.

A girl twelve years of age presented such a dirty unkempt appearance that the woman refused her. At the end of the day the child was presented again. Nobody would take her in. The woman had compassion on her and gave her shelter. The child was nervous, dirty and badly clad. She wet the bed the first night and was terrified of the consequences.[8]

Inevitably, there were tensions between rural householders and the evacuees billeted on them. For many children, the trauma was greatest where they had been completely uprooted from both their homes and their mothers; but the tensions were greatest where the mothers travelled with the children. To their shame, many newspapers published reports critical of the evacuees, totally uncomprehending of the appalling slum conditions which had created their predicament.

In a private report Mass Observation listed the main causes of tension as: the bad health of the evacuees, vermin, dirt, odd and rude behaviour, clothing, food problems, trouble with the children's mothers and money difficulties – in some cases, of course, the evacuees actually were better off than the people they were billeted on. Evacuation stories are rife, but they all contain some terrible truths about British society as it was in 1939.

One boy said he never went to sleep lying down, he perched himself by the bed post and went to sleep clinging to it with his head resting on it. . . .

One boy, 13, refused to eat cereal and milk, saying, 'I want some bloody beer and some chips.'[9]

Yet, even before the end of 1939, some social workers were drawing rather different lessons from the evacuation experience, maintaining that, even under these unfavourable circumstances, the mixing of social classes, and the mixing of town children with rural households, was providing the basis for more constructive social policies in the future. An original view of evacuation was presented by a retired naval commander of aristocratic outlook, writing to a business associate in the United States:

The tremendous social experiment of shifting the town population to the country has revealed, as far any how as the mothers and children are concerned, that country people – living in many cases round the Manors as in the old feudal days – are, though much poorer in worldly monetary wealth, infinitely richer in standards or cleanliness, happiness, kindliness, comfort and contentment than the towns folk. What does America with its contempt of feudalism say to this?[10]

Some children adapted happily to country life, but almost all missed their home surroundings, and particularly welcomed the visits from their parents (*Plate 12*). Since there were no bomb-attacks yet, by January 1940 more than half of the official evacuees had returned home. Meantime, in the period preceding and following the outbreak of war, at least two million other people had carried out their own private evacuation. Some children were sent out to Canada and other places – till the sinking of an evacuee ship brought a tragic ending to that.

4 Black-out, Gas Masks and Sandbags

Also on 1 September came the black-out. After thirty years of peace it is perhaps difficult to recall that one of the most characteristic features of the domestic front was the implacable darkness. In the first months, before the necessary adaptations were made, the black-out proved a bigger menace to civilian lives than the European war: there was a doubling in the number of road casualties (*Plate 18*). Sandbags and other accoutrements of war were much in evidence (*Plate 13*).

Yet the sense of unreality, the sense of continuity with the thirties, was maintained by the fact that at the end of 1939, as we have seen, there were still about a million men unemployed. Cinemas and theatres closed; but after a fortnight the cinemas were opened again; then, over the following weeks, the theatres cautiously began to reopen. Football

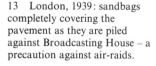

13 London, 1939: sandbags completely covering the pavement as they are piled against Broadcasting House – a precaution against air-raids.

14 'Wartime scholars, 22nd September 1939'; the caption to this photograph, taken by John Topham, continues: 'a lesson in progress at a Central School in north Kent, where schools have just been reopened by the Kent Education Committee. As the picture shows, scholars must take and keep their gas masks by them.'

15 Gas-driven car seen in London traffic after filling up with gas at a Hyde Park gas depot, April 1940.

and other spectator sports, banned at first because of the fear of the damage to morale from a bomb-attack on a place of public assembly, were also soon resumed (though with crowds limited to fifty per cent of normal to facilitate speedy exit to air-raid shelters). But, whereas cinemas and theatres were crowded, football never regained its former popularity during the war, mainly because of the reduced standards necessarily presented by the depleted teams. Schools reopened again after the immediate evacuation crisis; and gas masks continued to be the fundamental luggage of war (*Plate 14*).

While it was 'business as usual' in so many respects, those whose cars had been such a prized possession in the 1930s did begin to feel the pinch of war. Petrol rationing was introduced in October 1939, so a number of alternative sources of fuel were tried (*Plate 15*). For the very rich the black-out was little more than a minor, and slightly exciting, interruption (*Plate 16*).

In the early months of 1940 there was much talk in the press of the 'creeping paralysis' affecting the British war effort under Neville Chamberlain's Government. In April came the German invasion of

16   London's nightclubs carry on during the black-out. Diners entering the air-raid shelter, Paradise Club, October 1939.

17 Air-raid in the Orkney Islands in which the first civilian killed was Jim Isbister, April 1940: moving furniture from the Isbister hamlet.

Scandinavia, followed by the failed attempt to land and maintain British troops in Norway. It was also in April that a German air-raid on the Orkney Islands caused the first British civilian casualty from air attack (*Plate 17*). Norway became the focal point for gathering discontents, and on 10 May Chamberlain's Conservative Government gave place to a National Coalition under Winston Churchill.

One of the first actions of the new Government was to pass an amended Emergency Powers (Defence) Act, by which 'all persons could be required to place themselves, their services, and their property' at the disposal of the Government as appeared 'to be necessary or expedient for securing the public safety, the defence of the Realm, the maintenance of public order', or for the efficient prosecution of the war and for the maintenance of 'supplies or services essential to the community'. During the rest of the war, direction and control of life and labour in Britain were probably more total and more efficient than in any other combatant country, save for the Soviet Union. Totalitarian control can fall heavily on individuals and on

18 Black-out casualties: two cars (one a police car) which crashed in the black-out into a bomb crater during a night raid over south London, September 1940. Understandably enough, there are no pictures available of black-out crashes before the coming of the Blitz.

groups, on individualists and eccentrics, as well as on genuine subversives. But, for all the obtuseness of bureaucracy, war legislation was generally administered with respect for the need to maintain civilian support. Churchill himself had a profoundly traditional respect for Parliament, which remained in session throughout the war. There was a truce between the main political parties, but by-elections continued to be held. As far as such things can be determined, most of the censorship and control seems to have had the support of most people.

5 After Dunkirk

At the very moment that Churchill was assuming power, there came Hitler's invasion of the Low Countries, followed quickly by the fall of France and the evacuation of British and French troops from Dunkirk. The rounding up of small craft from many parts of the country in preparation for the Dunkirk evacuation had given some intimation to domestic society of what was going on; the return of 'the little boats' brought the message home (*Plate 19*).

An even more powerful message was conveyed by the sight of the men returning from Dunkirk, weary and often seriously wounded. At this time Nurse K. M. Phipps was working with staff from University College Hospital, London, in the Emergency Medical Services Hospital set up in the beautiful house and grounds of Ashridge Manor (the temporary huts in the grounds, now a depository of the Public Record Office, contain some of the most interesting documents consulted in the preparation of this book). She noted in her diary:

All our off duty had been cancelled, and around lunchtime a whole lot of ARP men with stretchers arrived and helpers from the village. . . . It was like standing on the stage waiting for the curtain to go up. One had perhaps over rehearsed and there was a horrid fear that it might suddenly turn into a quite different play, with a plot which was unfamiliar and lines which would have to be improvised. How right a hunch as it turned out!

Our staff nurse was a bit jittery, her fiancé was with the BEF [British Expeditionary Force], and some nasty rumours had been floating around to the effect that they were being evacuated under fire! But nobody knew anything definite. . . . Then a car drew up.

Two officers got out, limping and were helped into ward 10. We were all standing outside the hut door in spite of sister's feeble suggestion that it would look better if we were inside! Then it dawned on us that indeed things were wrong. . . . The officers were dirty, and untidy, one lacked a uniform coat the other had a bloody sling on his arm. Surely after going thru the regular Army casualty routine someone would have cleaned them up! They looked as if they had come straight off the battlefield . . . but we were not a first field dressing post we were a base hospital . . . the terminal point in fact. What could have happened!

Then the green line buses arrived and started to unload, they were mostly stretcher cases, so the ARP men were kept busy. But they wore beards, and there were thomas splints stuck out at all angles and blood stained head bandages. They all looked so dirty and did they smell! I was glad Sister had

19 The 'little boats' return from Dunkirk: Sunday afternoon strollers at Richmond waving to thirty of the boats towed by a tug, 9 June 1940.

20 Soldiers back from Dunkirk at a station in Kent, June 1940.

warned us about the stench of dried blood. We wanted to smile a welcome but felt nearer crying.

What little uniform they had was in a bad state, we had to cut it off in most cases. 'Down the seams nurse, it may have to be used again!' We found some of the wounds had field dressings still on that had stuck, and had to be soaked off. Their feet were in a bad state from marching and socks too had to be cut off. My scissors got so blunt in cutting through the heavy khaki, that in the end it was like sawing, but somehow we got them undressed. Sister and staff attended to the worst cases, and the volunteer helpers were put on to making tea, we were thankful for their assistance, and the little bags of 'comforts' were temporarily abandoned. I was glad that some had contained shaving sticks. Some men had to be cleaned up for the theatre and all of course needed urgent 'bottles', which the VADs [Volunteer Aid Detachments – established in 1910 and very prominent in the First World War, they were in effect nurses and orderlies] attended to in an efficient manner.

The men seemed dead tired, and we had to wash many asleep.

The stretchers came in pretty fast and then there was a lull. Some of us were sent to get a cup of tea, I remember an auxiliary fireman (who was stretcher bearing) said 'This brings the war a darn sight too close I wonder what the hell is happening over there.' He also had discovered that this was a convoy from Calais. . . . One thought he had come via Dunkirk . . . others said they had been anything up to a week getting here. One was terribly bad and sister said it was doubtful if he would live the night and arranged for relatives to be sent for. He lacked a foot and had terrible stomach wounds. Another had a fracture of the femur and shrapnel wounds all over and is also 'behind screens'. . . .

Pathetic little bits of equipment came in with the men . . . an army making a planned withdrawal doesn't send its wounded home in that condition, neither do men abandon their equipment![11]

Churchill did not attempt to dress up Dunkirk as anything other than a defeat: it was abundantly clear that the war for survival had truly begun, and that invasion might come at any time. The Home Front seemed to inch a little closer towards becoming a War Front as signposts and place-names were removed or painted out in order to confuse the potential invader (*Plate 21*), and defences were erected

21 Painters obliterating the nameplate at a railway station to avoid giving help to possible invaders, 11 June 1940.

22 Coastal defence: camouflaged communication trenches being built, July 1940.

along the country's coast-lines (*Plates 22 and 23*). It became an offence to leave a car unlocked, or a bicycle not immobilized, or to do anything else which might in any way help a German parachutist. Civilian movement was severely restricted in the whole south coast 'Defence Area'.

In actual fact there was a good deal of confusion in government circles over the best tactics to be adopted in the event of an invasion taking place. Most of the practical arrangements were in the hands of Local Invasion Committees. Official confusion spilled over into the press; on one famous occasion the Beaverbrook morning paper, the *Daily Express*, indicated that in the event of an invasion, people were to

23 Beach at Frinton, protected by barbed wire and guarded by the Royal Scottish Fusiliers, 7 September 1940. Perhaps this picture, taken by an army photographer, deliberately stressed the civilian nonchalance of the bathers.

evacuate themselves from the danger areas, whereas that same evening the Beaverbrook evening paper, the *Evening Standard*, strongly urged that in the event of an invasion people should stay where they were. The latter was in fact the policy on which the Government settled: the fall of France, it was felt, had been hastened by the manner in which vital roads were jammed with refugees. Churchill, however, strongly objected to the first slogan put to him, 'Stay Put', which he saw as unnecessarily defeatist. Instead, therefore, the Government came up with 'Stay Where You Are' and 'Stand Firm'. In the summer of 1940 two leaflets were issued to all householders, 'Stay Where You Are' and 'If the Invader comes'.

One may have doubts about the potential effectiveness of some of these preparations, particularly the removal and painting out of signs, but there can be no doubt that to the British people invasion had become a real possibility. One old gardener in an east Suffolk village, a soldier of the previous war, nevertheless declared:

A fella from London was down here last week and he asked me if we weren't afraid of being invaded. I said that's an insult to the British navy. As long as we've got that they'll never get here. . . .
Our air force is doing fine work, sir, and there's one thing we don't do, we don't bomb civilians like the Germans. It's hard luck to be killed like that. . . . It's so wrong if you haven't done nothing to anyone.[12]

Refugees, Jewish and non-Jewish, from Hitler's vicious regime had arrived in Britain during the later thirties. The German breakthrough in the west brought another influx of refugees, mostly from Belgium. It would be wrong to think of the British as being universally tolerant of the newcomers in their midst. The best one lady proprietor of a small sweet shop in Paddington could say of the Belgians was:

If they are anything like the Belgians in the last war – they are a dirty lot . . . but poor things they can't help it. I mean the Irish are dirty but we don't hate them. That's only the way they've been brought up.[13]

With the first invasion scare there came a much more ruthless approach towards aliens. In September 1939 known Nazi sympathizers and one or two others had been rounded up. From May to July 1940 there was an intensive campaign against all aliens of German or Austrian origin, and indeed against many others besides. Men were hastily rounded up and herded into camps in preparation for being deported to the Dominions. The papers of Sir Walter Monckton, at this time Deputy Director General of the Ministry of Information, contain contemporary accounts of one of the internment camps, in the former Prime Minister's constituency of Huyton. Food and living conditions were repellent; Nazis and anti-Nazis were mixed up together; men were suddenly seized without warning for deportation overseas. An inmate wrote: 'The two men who succeeded in committing suicide had already been in Hitler's concentration camps.

Against these they held out, but this camp has broken their spirit.' An observer from outside wrote: 'In outward appearance I am sure a concentration camp couldn't be worse.'[14] In the Liddell Hart Papers there is a very full and moving account, by the former head of the music school at Dartington Hall, of conditions at the Paignton Camp and at one he was subsequently sent to in Shropshire.[15]

There were violent attacks on aliens in the press, and public-opinion polls and Mass Observation showed that there was considerable popular sentiment against them. When Italy joined the war on the fall of France, Italian fish-and-chip shops and ice-cream parlours throughout the country were attacked. However, action in the House of Commons, particularly directed against the Home Secretary, Sir John Anderson, produced an easing of conditions and a gradual release of aliens towards the end of the year.

Dunkirk had its positive effects too. There was an immediate response to the government call for suspension of all holidays; late-coming and absenteeism practically vanished; phenomenally long hours were worked; productivity soared. Effects were temporary. Longer hours, as the First World War had amply demonstrated, do not – over a period – yield higher productivity. But the Dunkirk spirit, though short lived, was real enough.

6 On Guard

A meeting at the War Office, the day after Churchill formed his Government, and while Hitler's forces were pouring through in the west, decided to set up a force of local defence volunteers. On 14 May Churchill's new War Secretary, Anthony Eden, spoke on the BBC Home Service about the threat of German parachutists. He then continued:

Since the war began the Government have received countless enquiries from all over the kingdom from men of all ages who are for one reason or another not at present engaged in military service, and who wish to do something for the defence of their country. Well, now is your opportunity.
    We want large numbers of such men in Great Britain, who are British subjects, between the ages of 17 and 65 . . . to come forward now and offer their services. . . . The name of the new Force which is now to be raised will be 'The Local Defence Volunteers'. . . . This name describes its duties in three words. . . . This is . . . a part-time job, so there will be no need for any volunteer to abandon his present occupation. . . . When on duty you will form part of the armed forces. . . . You will not be paid, but you will receive a uniform and will be armed. . . .

Within twenty-four hours, a quarter of a million men had enlisted. To begin with, neither arms nor uniforms were forthcoming, so that the LDV often presented a disconcertingly amateurish appearance. It is probably for this reason that some of the earliest pictures of the LDVs were suppressed by the censor (*Plate 24*). The spirit, in the beginning, was somewhat haphazard (school cadets could be detailed

24 One of the earliest pictures of Local Defence Volunteers. Stamped by the censor 'not to be published'.

25 Cadets as guards. Cadets from a Midlands school, evacuated to the country, took their turn at guard duty with the local school OTC (Officers' Training Corps) during the day. Odham's Press photograph passed by the censor.

26 How to shoot down a dive bomber: the Home Guard learns the 'latest tricks of modern war'. Associated Press photograph, for first publication in evening papers, Tuesday 13 August 1940, and daily papers the next day. The somewhat unrealistic caption reads: 'Home Guard men now taking an intensive course in modern, realistic methods of warfare are seen here learning how to deal with dive bombers. This picture was taken at Osterley Park Home Guard Training School where ingenious apparatus – seen clearly in this picture – has been devised to swing a model bomber down in a realistic dive over the heads of gunners, who "blaze away" at it with their rifles.'

for guard duty, without being formally enrolled in the new organization [*Plate 25*]), or, depending on one's point of view, delightfully democratic – though behind the apparently informal style lay, as several commentators noted, a fundamentally 'feudal' system of recruitment to the officer class.[16]

Winston Churchill first used the name 'Home Guard' in a broadcast of 14 July, and this became the formal title of the new organization on 23 July 1940. On 6 August 1940 came the so-called 'Magna Carta of the Home Guard', which began the process of properly integrating it into the Army. In November the 'provisional' character of the Home Guard was to be given 'more permanent shape'; it was now to have commissioned officers, NCOs, and a fixed organization.

The functions of the Home Guard were both very real, since parachutists and a seaward invasion were genuinely expected, and unreal, since the invasion did not in fact materialize, and since some of the Guard's activities seem rather remote from the true realities of war (*Plate 26*). It is in a way ironical that the Home Guard is often said to have been at its period of greatest importance during the time when an invasion was a possibility, although it was never called upon to deal with such an invasion, whereas later, when it performed many other very valuable tasks, such as aircraft spotting, guarding of bomb-sites and so on, it was held to have passed its period of glory. In British social history, the real importance of the Home Guard was the sense which it gave to many citizens, who also retained their normal civilian employment, of complete involvement in all aspects of the war effort. This was true too of the other part-time posts created to deal with the new dangers of total war, such as air-raid warden and fire watcher.

Mrs Brinton-Lee, whose husband was a Major in the Home Guard, wrote a sensitive, if slightly patronizing description of her husband's men:

They were most of them elderly, with kind, careworn faces. I thought how nice they were, neither bombastic or craven, like the Germans I had met. They had done their job in the last war, as their ribbons showed; they had worked and worried and raised their families. The things they were interested in were good things, – their work, their hobbies, their children and their sport. They had no inferiority complex, they had never gone hysterical or wished to take away anybody's freedom. Their only crime was that, being unable to believe that the rest of the world was crazy, they had been rather inclined to let things slide. They did not know how to spell Czechoslovakia, or where it was, and they had been only too willing to believe that Europe was no concern of their's. Now, when they found everything had come unstuck, they turned up quite cheerfully, and offered themselves and their services again. They were tough and uncomplaining. I was sure they would fight like tigers when it came to the point, and meanwhile they practised their drill and shooting in the friendliest way, and went home to be with their families through the night's hell, till it was time to go to work in the morning.[17]

7 The Battle of Britain

Air activity began around Dover on 10 July, but it was not till August that the Germans definitively embarked on the attempted destruction of the RAF and its bases, as a preliminary to the intended invasion. On 8 August the RAF shot down thirty-one German planes, while the Luftwaffe tally was twenty British, though Eagle Day, the one set for the beginning of the systematic destruction of Fighter Command in the air and on the ground, was set for 13 August. Actually, the day of maximum German effort was 15 August, when the Luftwaffe flew nearly 1,800 sorties. Sixty-two civilians were killed in the vicinity of Croydon airport. On the 17th more bombs fell on south London, and on the 18th there was another massive attack. These raids were all successfully beaten off with disproportionate losses being inflicted on the Germans. But on 24 August there began the most desperate fortnight of all. The terms of battle began to swing against Britain, with, in particular, a frighteningly high loss of pilots. The Germans came very near to destroying the vital ring of seven sector-stations round London.

It was on 20 August that Churchill made that so often quoted speech in the House of Commons: 'Never in the field of human conflict was so much owed by so many to so few.' The phrase has been much parodied since, and it is said that even at the time one fighter pilot himself remarked: 'That must refer to Mess bills.' Dr Calder has remarked that, 'never had so many warriors owed so much to so many.' Certainly, the ground crews, the women of the WAAF, the civilian repair units, and, of course, the workers in the aircraft factories, all played a vital part. At the time, the British people knew nothing of radar – hence the stories about pilots eating carrots in order to see in the dark – but that too, together with the whole armoury of modern technology, played its part. Already in existence, and ready for battle, were the volunteers of the Royal Observer Corps, the civilians of the Post Office War Group, the Home Guards, the VADs and the nurses in the emergency hospitals.

Yet, though in the end the war was won by an entire people, the actual fighting of this particular battle was indeed conducted by a tiny élite minority. Most came from upper-class homes, though they had developed a special tradition of their own, somewhat at odds with that of the older military caste. We have all seen film, actual or re-created, of the fighter pilots scrambling to their planes at a moment's notice. Their lives were impossible: flying as many as half-a-dozen sorties a day, they often had to go back into the skies totally exhausted or even wounded. A freshly trained squadron could be shattered after ten days active service. As one pilot said: 'We were dead. We were too tired even to get drunk. You simply never saw a pilot drunk.' *Plate 27* perhaps says as much as any of the better-known pictures. It was obviously un-set-up and un-composed, as one can see from the untidy hand with a glass in the top left-hand corner. One can well believe, too, that the holder of that glass fell asleep long before he had time to have another drink.

Although German objectives in the Battle of Britain were primarily military, there were many civilian casualties from Orkney (as we have seen) to Aberdeen (where more than fifty people were killed or seriously injured on 12 July), to parts of the Midlands, south London, and above all Hampshire and the Dover region. Air-raid sirens and air-

27 1940: RAF pilots, almost continually in the air, took short naps between raids, so as to be ready to go at a moment's notice. Unpublished photograph, taken for the *Kent Messenger*.

Opposite:
28   The Battle of Britain: dog fight over Sidcup, aircraft vapour trails.

29   Scene at Dover during air-raid, September 1940. A barrage balloon is shot down. Picture printed in *Illustrated*.

30   Battle of Britain: soldiers on guard over a shot-down Nazi plane, a Junker 88, 1940.

31   Battle of Britain: first-aid for the pilot of a Messerschmitt 109, who landed in south-east England after bailing out of his machine, which was shot down in flames, 29 August 1940.

raid shelters were now in constant use; and even if in fact people were not in any direct danger, the nuisance value of enemy attacks was very high. Those living near air bases were particularly aware of what was going on, and those living in the Midlands could often hear British fighter pilots roaring overhead, just as those in the far south could hear the enemy planes coming in.

People in the south could watch the air battles going on over their heads, though these were difficult to photograph, and often all that could actually be seen were the vapour trails of the aircraft (*Plate 28*). Sometimes all the raiders managed to achieve was the shooting down of a barrage balloon (*Plate 29*).

The rest of the country had listened to the BBC commentaries which, in rather ghoulish fashion, tended to present the life-and-death aerial combat as a species of sporting contest. This fashion was apparently set almost by accident by BBC commentator Charles Gardner, when he happened to be on the spot at Dover on 10 July. His off-the-cuff broadcast ran:

There's one coming down in flames – there somebody's hit a German – and he's coming down – there's a long streak – he's coming down completely out of control – a long streak of smoke – ah, the man's bailed out by parachute – the pilot's bailed out by parachute – he's a Junker 87 and he's going slap into the sea and there he goes – sma-a-ash . . . Oh boy, I've never seen anything so good as this – the R.A.F. fighters have really got these boys taped.

News vendors entered into the sporting spirit by chalking up such headlines as: 'Biggest raid ever – score 78–26 – England still batting.' The totals were greatly exaggerated.

German pilots who bailed out over land could often be expected to be mercilessly pursued by members of the Home Guard, though traditions of chivalry towards a fallen foe often revived when a pilot's pathetic condition was realized (*Plate 31*). Incinerated wreckage strewn about the fields and downs also drove home the sense of Britain now being in the Front Line. Aircraft had to be carefully guarded from, among others, eager souvenir hunters (*Plate 30*).

On 24 August, German pilots by mistake bombed central London, contrary to Hitler's specific instructions. RAF bombers were therefore sent against Berlin. For the first time the Germans instituted deliberate attacks on British civilian cities: Liverpool was bombed on the nights of 28, 29, 30 and 31 August, with serious fires being started in its commercial centre on the last night. At five o'clock on the afternoon of Saturday 7 September, a glorious summer day, the deliberate mass attack on the East End of London began. Civilians were now right bang in the middle of the war.

CHAPTER THREE

The Blitz: 1940–41

1 The Blitz on the East End

The bombs poured down on the dock areas of West Ham and Bermondsey, and on adjoining Poplar, Shoreditch, Whitechapel and Stepney. This was the Stepney of the 1939 rent strikes; this was the East End of violent clashes between Fascists and Communists, this was the East End of mixed races, of very ordinary people and of humble homes. 'The Pool, below London Bridge, was a lake of light. . . . Half a mile or more of the Surrey shore was burning' . . . 'the whole bloody world's on fire', said the fire officer in charge at the Surrey docks, where 250 acres of timber had been set alight. There were rubber fires, paint fires, rum fires and even pepper fires, all creating their own explosions and their own type of stinging or asphyxiating smoke. All night more and more incendiary and high-explosive bombs poured down on the flaming docks and streets. The fires could be seen for 30 miles.

Firemen, and the various auxiliary and voluntary services, fought heroically, but the authorities simply were not prepared for anything like this. Firemen were filthy, weary, red-eyed, choked and, sometimes, cut off and burnt to death. ARP workers struggled to clear away rubble and bring out the dazed and half-suffocated occupants buried beneath. WVS workers sought to get families away from the stricken streets. Thousands of homes were destroyed; 430 civilians were killed and 1,600 were seriously injured. The bombers returned at eight o'clock on the Sunday evening; another 400 civilians were killed.

On the Monday morning (9 September) the press brought out its own version. A leader-page article in the *Daily Herald*, written by star journalist Hannen Swaffer, read:

East London paused, for a moment yesterday, to lick its wounds after what had been planned by Hitler as a night of terror.
But it carried on.
During a five-hour tour of the bombed area, I met only one disgruntled person – a youth who complained that in his district there were not enough shelters.

The Times said:

These people had been through a terrible experience. Many had had narrow escapes. Many were homeless. But their general verdict was that the endurance

Opposite:
32 The Blitz, September 1940: the East End on fire.

33 Surrey docks and warehouse blaze, 7–8 September 1940. This photograph was taken for the *News Chronicle*, but stopped by the censor.

34 Beaconsfield, October 1940. London refugees from the Blitz wait for a bus to take them to their billets. Picture taken for *Illustrated*.

35 Beaconsfield, October 1940. London refugees buying food and clothing from barrowmen. Picture taken for *Illustrated*.

of such an experience was an incident in the process of winning the mastery over a ruthless enemy; and that they were not going to flinch until that mastery was won.

But the facts, as a secret Mass Observation report put it, were rather different. From early on Monday morning a steady stream of people were leaving the area, as much as 60 per cent in some streets, though certainly mainly older people.

Of course, the press versions of life going on normally in the East End on Monday are grotesque. There was no bread, no electricity, no milk, no gas, no telephones. There was thus every excuse for people to be distressed.... There was no understanding in the huge buildings of Central London for the tiny crumbled streets of densely massed population. Here, people wanted to be brave but found bravery was something purely negative, cheerless, and without encouragement or prospect of success.[18]

Another Mass Observation report noted:

Nobody foresaw the tidal wave of refugees spread all over the country after the first hideous week-end, inundating places like Oxford with homeless people, being decanted in peaceful Essex suburbs from lorries by desperate local authorities who hoped for the best that something would be done about them. Nobody foresaw that everybody would not know all about the official plans for them, that the rest centres would be overflowing, that people would stay there for weeks instead of hours, that people would not be able to be billeted in their own boroughs, that transport would not turn up, so that refugees were bombed to death in the rest centres, that people would flock to the tubes and unofficial deep shelters rather than use the official surface shelters which they regarded as death traps. In fact, there were rather too many things that nobody foresaw for official democracy to plume itself very much on its efficiency as a wager of war on the Home Front.[19]

In some cases, people spent days on end in Green Line coaches, since there was simply nowhere to dump them. A lady wrote from Oxford: 'There are over 27,000 evacuees from the east side of London, and it is very pathetic to see them wandering about the streets here – in many cases absolutely unwanted and miserable.'[20]

Bombs, too, starkly exposed the shoddy construction of the mean little streets which had housed the population of the East End. It did not always need a direct hit to flatten these houses as a tiny breath would flatten a house of cards (*Plate 37*).

2 The Nation in the Front Line

Just as London was beginning in October to adapt to its front-line situation, the air attacks on the provinces began to expand and intensify. There was a heavy raid on Birmingham on 25 October, but then on 14 November a new phase began with the total devastation of the whole of the centre of Coventry (where there had been one or two small raids in October, sufficiently serious to encourage some citizens to move out into the commuter areas of the Warwickshire country-side).

36 Londoners wait outside a 'tunnel shelter' an unofficial deep shelter, 26 September 1940.

37 9 September 1940, houses in Stepney damaged by the previous night's raids: *News Chronicle* photograph stopped by the censor. The photograph reveals very clearly the devastating effects of blast on the jerry-built terraced houses of the East End. It is not surprising that all such pictures were suppressed by the censor.

38 Evacuating families the day after the 14 November 1940 air-raid on Coventry. Published in *Illustrated*, February 1941.

The immediate situation was as desperate as that during the first weekend raid on the East End of London.

The night of 14 November was cold and clear, with the hard frost sparkling in the moonlight readily perceptible to the four men fire-watching on the roof of the famous Gothic cathedral. The Central Control at Coventry received the yellow warning at seven o'clock and the red warning ten minutes later. Soon after the planes were overhead, first dropping flares attached to parachutes, then incendiary bombs with explosive charges, then landmines and high-explosive bombs. By twenty-four minutes past seven the first fires in the centre of Coventry were being reported. The 'raiders passed' signal did not come till sixteen minutes past six on the morning of 15 November. Four hundred planes had dropped 30,000 incendiaries and 500 tons of bombs and landmines; nearly 50,000 houses had been damaged, with 20,000 rendered totally uninhabitable; three-quarters of the city's industry was affected; telephones, water, electricity and gas supplies were totally disrupted; the tramway system was rendered unusable and 156 buses out of a fleet of 181 were put out of action. Two hundred firemen were injured while fighting the fires and 26 lost their lives; 865 civilians were seriously injured, 554 were killed.

The devastation of a relatively small town could be much worse in its effects than that of parts of London; Londoners, at least, could always move to other parts of the great metropolis, where shops and services were still functioning. For a time, it seemed as if the whole of Coventry

Opposite:
39 Sorting personal property after the German air-raid on Coventry of 14 November 1940. *Illustrated* photograph, not published until February 1941.

40 Trekking from Southampton, December 1940. The caption which accompanied the published picture in the *News Chronicle* perhaps put a more cheerful face on events than the picture itself warrants: 'On the right are children and women waiting on a main road for a lift. Those made homeless in the heavy raids have been distributed over surrounding reception areas. In the streets of Southampton mobile canteens serve cups of tea and light meals. By last night provision had been made for nearly all the homeless people.'

had been put totally out of action. Six hundred soldiers were drafted into the city to help with demolition, clearing the streets and keeping order. *Plate 39*, which was not published till February 1941, seems to suggest some tension between neighbours, which is the other side of the usual coin on which resolute citizens present unflinching unity in the face of adversity. Soon there were over a thousand soldiers in Coventry, and, in addition, 1,200 slaters and other building workers were released from the Army. Shops and food supplies were in chaos, and army field-kitchens were in action first before the Womens' Volunteer Service began to take over. For the first ten days those shops which were still open were asked to keep their sales close to normal, but not to insist on seeing ration books. Incoming supplies were diverted, since they could not be used; instead the citizens of Coventry got a special issue of tinned corned beef from the Ministry of Food. After a week, an effective Communal Feeding Centre was established.

41 More Southampton trekkers, December 1940. Again the *News Chronicle* caption was relatively cheerful: 'Southampton refugees on their way out of the town to a new home.'

Devastating attacks, sometimes repeated more than once, followed on Birmingham, Southampton, Manchester, Sheffield, Portsmouth and Leicester. In every case, one of the first symptoms was the tide of refugees, or 'trekkers', leaving for the surrounding countryside (*Plates 40 and 41*).

Everywhere, the firemen (*Plate 42*) performed heroically, and gradually, as in London, led by the auxiliary and voluntary services, the authorities and the public made some kind of adaptation to the new situation.

Meantime, the raids on London, broadening out to cover the West End and the suburbs, as well as the East End, continued for seventy-six consecutive nights, save for 2 November when bad weather kept the raiders at bay. There were daytime raids as well, which were dangerous and disruptive, but it was the night raids which brought terror and devastation.

42 Firemen in action during a
night raid on Manchester, 23
December 1940.

43 Bombed-out Liverpool
family outside a reception
centre. This photograph,
passed by the censor, was given
a chirpy caption: 'Are they
down hearted? Blitztown: a
Liverpool family, bombed out
of their home, rest outside a
reception centre and wonder
what they will do next. But
there is no sign of sinking
spirits, just a good natured
acceptance of fate.'

Opposite:
44 1940 Blitz on Bexley, Kent.

45   St Paul's in the Blitz, 29 December 1940. This has been described by Dr Calder as 'the classic photographic image of the blitz', and by the photographic agency as 'one of the war's greatest pictures'.

On the Sunday night a large public shelter in Beaufort Street had received a direct hit. There were no survivors, and as soon as it got light on Monday morning, the ambulance girls from the adjacent post were sent to help the rescue and demolition squad to remove the human remains. They had to put what they could collect into blue waterproof bags and take them to the mortuary. [One volunteer nurse] had seen a man pick up a head and put it into the sack, and another with his hand scrape a woman's scalp off the surface of a concrete block, where it had stuck when the head was smashed against it. She had seen a half-born dead baby attached to its dead mother.[21]

On 29 December came the famous attack on the City of London, when the Thames was at low ebb so that there was a great shortage of water, and when St Paul's itself somehow managed to rise unscathed among the flames all around it. The fires continued for days. The attitude of a landowner, businessman and property developer, who had kept away from his city office during the height of the Blitz, expressed in a letter to his nephew in the Sudan Political Service, is illuminating:

It is of course infuriating that Wren Churches and the Guildhall and City Livery Companies Halls should be destroyed or mauled about but we shall ultimately not regret the destruction of piles of antiquated buildings in the St. Pauls area. No legislation could have got rid of them without hideous sums of compensation and yet most of them were antiquated, many partially empty, and few of them susceptible to modernisation, as I well know from being a director of the Sackville Estate which has had a number of properties rised [sic] to the ground.[22]

Opposite:
46   General view of bomb-damaged City of London, taken from the top of St Paul's Cathedral, 3 January 1941.

47 Bank Underground collapse. The *News Chronicle* caption, when the picture was released in January 1942, read: 'Twelve months ago a bomb fell in the roadway near the Bank of England – this is one view of the damage it did. The censor released these pictures yesterday. So that the traffic might continue to use this busy crossing Royal Engineers constructed a temporary bridge across the crater. The underground subway caved in, the booking hall was destroyed, a number of people were killed.'

In the London area, some of the worst individual disasters were caused by bombs falling on crowded tube stations. Henry Penny's contemporary diary reveals that people were well aware that several hundred were drowned when a bomb severed water pipes at Balham tube station. Reports, and photographs, of these incidents, of course, were not published at the time. When the Bank underground station was bombed in January 1941, 111 people were killed; the censor did not release pictures of this for another twelve months, and even then the main purpose was to show the way in which a temporary bridge enabled this busy road junction to be kept in operation (*Plate 47*).

The heaviest raids of all, both on London and on other great centres of population, took place throughout the spring of 1941 – the west Midlands, including Coventry again, suffered devastating raids on 8, 9 and 10 April, and Merseyside had a terrible eight nights, its 'May week', at the beginning of that month. In March 1941 it was the turn of Clydeside, where, perhaps, continuing bitterness between employers and employed had remained strongest, and where there was still a great sense of remoteness from the war. Almost every house in the shipbuilding town of Clydebank was damaged. In the aftermath, the

48 Clydeside Blitz, 19 March 1941. 'Bombed tenement houses are still smoking ruins. Picture made after Thursday and Friday night's raid on Clydeside, in which 500 people were killed, and 800 injured.'

local Director of Education (J. P. McHutchison) toured the town with the Provost and a local Labour Member of Parliament, David Kirkwood. McHutchison noted in his diary:

It was all too pathetically evident that terrific damage to houses had been done, especially in the Parkhall and north Kilbowie Housing Schemes, and in the poorest working-class areas of Crown Avenue, and First and Second Avenues, in which streets the miles of four-storey tenements had been completely gutted by fire; some parts were still blazing and hundreds of the tenants watching from piles of saved furniture the holocaust of their homes. Long queues of now homeless folks awaited the buses that would take them away, and Drumry Road was black with men, women and children waiting at the church Rest Centre for food and guidance. It was a sad, sad sight, relieved however and glorified by uncomplaining fortitude and brave resignation. . . .

The contrast between the ugliness of ruination by man's hand and the beauty of warm Spring days will live ever in one's memory, as will the grand courage of so heavily stricken people: not a sign of panic or hysteria anywhere, though almost all were now homeless and thousands had lost their all. . . .

Clydebank has had a bad knock, probably severer than Coventry or any English town, since the whole town 'got it' and no single area or district escaped. It is quite plain that the object was to block out the whole place and thereby close down all work at Browns R.O.F. [Royal Ordnance Factory] and

Singers. (Curiously enough no fatal damage was done at any of these places, Browns especially receiving hardly any damage.) But that object has not been achieved, for early in this week Browns and Singers have been almost as busy as before, and folks are beginning to trickle back to the less severely damaged houses, and windowless and battered shops to commence trading. No praise is too great for the people: even amongst those who have lost their homes for the duration of the war or have lost as so many have all their earthly possessions, there has been no complaining: and the rest centres in the Vale of Leven and country districts, though pitiful enough scenes there were, have been gladdened by the mutual helpfulness and consideration of everybody, and their appreciation of what was being done for them.[23]

3 Rich and Poor: Government and Governed

Although there is much evidence, as in the long extract just quoted, of upper- and middle-class praise for the stoicism and heroism of the workers, there is really very little hard evidence of a genuine mixing of the social classes. On the whole, middle-class observers were horrified by the squalor they saw in the early days of resort to the tube stations, and in the large public shelters. Some large shelters, indeed, acquired a horrifying reputation for their sordid, insanitary condition. Many of the very rich continued to lead very segregated existences. The first shelter census of November 1940 showed that, of the 40 per cent who resorted to shelters, 27 per cent used their own domestic shelters and that only 9 per cent used public shelters; 4 per cent resorted to the tubes. There are numerous personal records of friendliness and social contact which seemed to transcend normal social barriers. But in part this can be explained by a need, in time of danger, to communicate freely, and avoid conditions of social isolation. Obviously, those caught suddenly in an air-raid could not afford to observe all the niceties of class distinction.

There are many fascinating overtones in the following two extracts of September 1940 from the diary of Hilda Neal, an upper-class lady living in London:

An aggressive Labour bus driver told me the East End people were saying their houses were destroyed, or allowed to be destroyed and no one cared; but when the West End was touched the government started the barrage!

Bruton Street, Bond Street, and Park Lane all bombed yesterday; much damage to the two former, but people are carrying on as usual. Milkman delivers slowly, pushing his tricycle during raid; the paper comes, and so on and so forth. Wonderful stoicism.

Three women Legion officers have been killed in East End; Mrs. Noel and the Misses Cooper; yesterday, while running a mobile canteen. Several firemen too; and two were blown over a building on an escape ladder, which was broken in half. One is just stunned to read of these happenings which often are beyond belief. Such heroism everywhere in all classes.

The Tube stations are filled with people packed together for the night. Wondered if I would join them, then concluded that even loneliness was best at *home*.[24]

49 Manchester Canal air-raid shelter: half-mile-long tunnel from Central Station to Water Street. *Illustrated*, 26 September 1940.

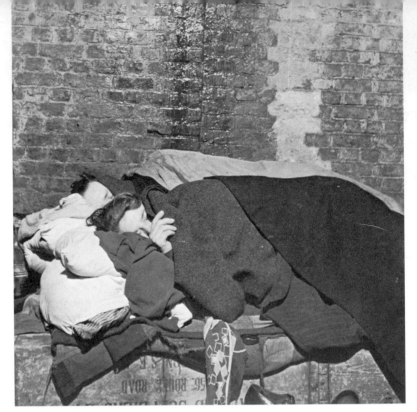

50 South-east London, 1940:
London shelterers sleeping near
a wall down which water is
running.

51 'Sheltered lives': *Illustrated*
picture, 1940. 'When the air-raid
warning sounds hairdressing still
continues in the underground
shelter at the West End London
establishment of T. Vasco Ltd.'

A kind of shelter life soon grew up, with its rules and conventions, though it is not surprising that many working-class activists and middle-class radicals thought that much shelter accommodation continued to be a disgrace to the authorities ostensibly responsible for providing it. Rapidly, shelter life became a matter of routine, and indeed of regulation. A shelter admission card, issued by the Borough of Islington in the London Civil Defence region, listed the holder's name, age, national registration number, full postal address, nature of employment, his signature, the name of the shelter, and his bunk number.

On the other side was the injunction:

READ THIS:

This ticket may be withdrawn at the Controller's discretion at any time and will be withdrawn if ANY of the following things happen: –

(a)   the shelter ceases to be available;

(b)   the holder of this ticket or any member of his family commits any offence or creates any nuisance or disturbance in the shelter, or fails to do his share in keeping the shelter tidy and clean;

(c)   this ticket is produced by any other than the registered holder;

(d)   the shelter is not used by the holder for four consecutive days without explanation;

(e)   the holder disregards any lawful order or request of a police officer, air-raid warden, shelter marshal or other authorised officer;

(f)   the holder fails to remove from the shelter all bedding and personal belongings as and when required for shelter cleaning purposes.

IF NOT OCCUPIED BY TWELVE MIDNIGHT BUNKS WILL NOT BE RESERVED FOR ABSENT TICKET-HOLDERS.

A rather different view is given by a pastoral letter written by the Methodist minister of Archway Central Hall in north London for the benefit of his far-flung flock: 'Our air-raid shelter is the most popular thing in north London at the moment! Large crowds gather outside it every night wanting to come in. It looks just like the pit entrance to a popular play, and we actually have queue artistes doing turns outside the Hall!' After commenting on high morale (and this was as early as 13 September 1940), the minister continues: 'The things some of them would do to Hitler if they got hold of him are unprintable in an Archway letter, but you can understand it.'[25]

The Government was much criticized for not getting on quickly enough with clearing up after the Blitzes. There were many difficulties, certainly, but these were made worse by the incompetence of the local authorities and the inefficiency of the small building firms. At the same time it was noted that, while civilians were suffering so much, soldiers were relatively well-off. The *Daily Telegraph* wittily suggested that the Army should be set to knitting socks and scarves for the civilians. There was also much pressure for troops to be used in helping to clear up. Sir

52 The Duke of Kent watching troops pulling down a wall of a damaged and unsafe building, 6 January 1941.

Opposite:
53 London restaurant, 1940 or 1941. 'You could still enjoy marvellous meals . . . provided you had the money. The biggest change in restaurants was in the clientele – far more people now in uniform.'

54 An Anderson shelter still standing amid the debris, while rescue parties search the wreckage, 14 February 1941.

Warren Fisher, the handsome, clever, athletic figure who had been head of the Civil Service and *éminence grise* behind British politics in the inter-war years, was appointed Special Commissioner – or 'Chief Clearer-upper', as the media called him. After twenty years in the shadows, Fisher proved remarkably good at promoting publicity for himself, but he was much less successful in securing the troops he demanded. Churchill was strongly against soldiers being used for civilian tasks, and Ernest Bevin, who thought Fisher an incompetent ass in any case, wanted only ordinary trade-union labour to be employed, though he hoped to draft such labour in from outside. The local authorities preferred to go on working through the small contractors they knew best. As it was, clearing up proceeded very slowly, and only a few troops were used (*Plate 52*).

In many respects, of course, the rich did join with the poor in a common experience of hardship and discomfort. However, the good life continued throughout the Blitz, and, curiously, no attempt seems to have been made to suppress photographs of, for instance, expensive restaurants (*Plate 53*).

Originally the main public shelters provided were surface brick shelters which were quite spectacularly useless and dangerous. For private householders the corrugated-iron Anderson shelter was available, but it was only of use for those who had gardens. Although liable to flooding, it was remarkably effective (*Plate 54*). Then the

55 The Morrison shelter. Mrs Churchill and Mr Herbert Morrison watch Miss Ellen Wilkinson (left) and three others try a Morrison air-raid shelter, 11 February 1941.

Opposite:
56 Queuing up for water at the Elephant and Castle, 11 May 1941. *News Chronicle* photograph stopped by the censor.

57 Ernest Bevin tours blitzed Humberside, 15 May 1941. 'Mr. Bevin on the rubble heap: Mr. Ernest Bevin shakes hands with blitzed householders as he tours Humberside. A considerable part of the Minister's tour took him over wreckage-strewn roads.'

Morrison shelter, suitable for putting inside working-class homes, was developed (*Plate 55*). *Plate 55*, a very carefully composed and set-up picture, is noteworthy for its attempt to present leading figures as being genuinely involved with this new people's shelter, and for its very stylized representation of unity in political leadership. Along with Mrs Churchill, we see Herbert Morrison, London Labour leader, and now Minister of Home Security in place of the unpopular Sir John Anderson, and Ellen Wilkinson, another prominent Labour politician, and formerly one of the leaders of the Jarrow Hunger Marches. In the ineffable political jargon of the seventies, Morrison would probably be termed a 'moderate' (perhaps Mrs Churchill, too: she was a truly charming and gracious lady), Ellen Wilkinson an 'extremist'.

Labour leaders, by this time, were closely involved in the running of the war, most particularly on the Home Front. The Blitz not only created new social problems, it laid starkly bare many old ones, as (for instance) the inadequacy of water supplies in such working-class areas as the Elephant and Castle in London (see *Plate 56* – no wonder the censor stopped this one). The Minister of Labour, Ernest Bevin, was the most powerful and brilliant trade-union leader of his generation; once known as 'the Docker's K.C.', he had been the genius behind the building up of the massive Transport and General Workers' Union, but he had never even been a Member of Parliament when Churchill brought him into government. Although Bevin's policies for the direction of labour were tough, his presence in the Government was some guarantee that the problems of the poorer sections would not be totally ignored (*Plate 57*).

4 Morale

By the early summer of 1941 the very worst of the Blitz was over, as Hitler turned his fury against the Soviet Union. Compared with the damage inflicted on German cities in the later stages of the war, total casualties do not seem to have been enormous, and indeed were a good deal less than government plans in the 1930s had predicted. None the less, at the time, the Blitz was severe in its effects. It was without precedent; and those in its midst had no means of knowing when, if ever, it would cease. Casualties had been over-estimated, but the Government and local authorities had drastically failed to plan for the destruction to property, and the resultant plight of the homeless and the need for ancillary services.

How did the British people react? Did bombing strengthen morale, consolidate support behind the British Government, and increase the determined hostility towards Germany? Or did morale come close to disintegration? Was there hostility to, and resentment against, government and authority everywhere?

The broad outlines are pretty clear. When an area was severely blitzed for the first time morale took quite a battering. But after the first shock, most people adapted remarkably quickly. Social psychologists make a useful distinction between 'active' and 'passive' morale. High 'active' morale, shown in heroic gestures, the painting of exuberant slogans and so on, was confined to a tiny minority. But the majority managed to muster sufficient 'passive' morale, a grim, if often baffled, willingness to carry on. And a handful of those with high 'active' morale helped to keep the majority going. There is often more than a touch of the newspaper headline about the diary of Henry Penny, the London bus driver, but the sentiment seems genuine enough:

Although the past week has been very Trying with Bombs and Sleepless nights we are still not 'Downhearted' for as it has been said. We are all in the 'Front Line' and we realise it.

Several Day 'Alerts'. Some for several Hours. But nobody takes the slightest 'Heed' of these 'Alerts'. All Traffic on the Streets and all businesses 'Carry On'.[26]

Tom Harrisson has pointed out that many of the accounts of exhilaration and heroism were written much later, and do not in fact tally with what the same people were writing at the time of the Blitz. On the other hand, there is a good deal of genuinely contemporary material, which does seem to show a clear sign of high morale. Among the many fine collections in the Imperial War Museum, it is the memoirs of E. Leslie Mann, a Sidcup schoolmaster, *written up twenty years later*, which lay most stress on faltering morale, the undercurrents of criticism of the authorities and the general joylessness of the whole experience. Hindsight, it seems, can operate both ways. The Cabinet had been desperately worried about morale in June 1940, before the Blitz began. Thereafter, the secret reports coming before the

War Cabinet, without being starry-eyed, give a favourable review of civilian reactions. A Memorandum by the Home Secretary, on air-raids during the period September to November 1940, began with a distinction which may be usefully linked with the one made by social psychologists between 'active' and 'passive' morale:

The effects of the raids can be considered as the transient and the durable. The transient effects were those on morale and general disorganization. London people lost much sleep and suffered anxiety and discomfort, but there was no breakdown, no panic and no mass evacuation, except in the small heavily bombed areas. The effect was one very largely of surprise. After a few days the first horror of the raids wore off and people became adjusted to the new conditions of shelter life.

Disorganization was more serious. The complicated network of railways was cut at many places at once. In three weeks, 104 railway bridges were put out of action for periods ranging from a day to a month. Roads were blocked by craters and debris. Thousands of water and gas mains were broken, interrupting supplies over large areas (4,124 water mains were broken in the three months raiding). Telephone exchanges were put out of action and postal deliveries hampered.

The Memorandum then goes on to stress the way in which the earlier raids were made much worse by the presence 'and even more by the imagined presence' of unexploded bombs, which 'effectively sterilized whole areas and multiplied the number of homeless to be dealt with'. The disorganization was at first cumulative, but, gradually, or so the Home Secretary optimistically maintained, it was overcome, partly because of the slackening of the raids, partly because of the way in which people were adjusting to raid conditions.[27]

All letters leaving Britain were read by the censorship; obviously this put some limitation on their reliability as sources for what people were really thinking: at the same time it meant that the Government did have direct insight into what people were writing in their letters abroad. On Churchill's personal instructions, this information was circulated to the War Cabinet. The compiler of the report noted that writers of such letters were consistent that they must continue to work, even during raids, otherwise their nerves would suffer in time; also that normal amusements must continue. He singled out this extract from a letter written from London's East End:

Wait till the boys of the bulldog breed go to work in a real way. They'll be biting chunks out of them Nazies till there's nothing left of 'em. Yes we're gonna pulverize 'em not criticise 'em.[28]

Some of the bias inevitable in this source is apparent in the statement that: 'Morale is highest in London, but the provinces run a good second, and only a few letters from Liverpool, mostly from Irish writers, show any sign of panic.'

Probably the fairest survey of all was the Civil Defence report No. 22, covering the period 1 September 1940 to 29 September 1940, submitted by the Minister of Home Security to the War Cabinet. While maintaining that 'morale continues to be good', this report did admit that the police were seriously concerned about the friction between the inhabitants of certain northern towns and unofficial evacuees who had fled from bombed areas in the south.[29]

One Mass Observation full-time investigator, on holiday at the time in the Midlands, latched on to some of the undertones of the friction between native Midlanders and London evacuees. The main trouble was over food, and it was alleged that evacuees and refugees were queueing up at nine o'clock outside shops and buying up vast quantities of food, leaving nothing for regular customers. More depressingly:

In Leicester after the air-raid, rumours spread that the Londoners, having run from one town, were running away again. There were no good words said for them at all. The words 'evacuees' and 'Jews' were used interchangeably; all those who have run away are thought to be Jews.[30]

Hilda Neal, in Kensington, had tended to take an unfavourable view of the morale of the East Enders.[31] But many private letters do tell a different story:

It makes me terribly sad to think of the appalling havoc that has been wrought in London. We could see the docks blazing from here or rather the terrific red glow in the sky. We have a refugee family from Wapping in an empty house in our road, they arrived about 7 o'clock last Friday night with bedding but practically nothing else. No black-out or anything done for them, all the neighbours rallied round and lent different things. But the woman was amazingly brave, she really staggered me, but she certainly proved that what the papers say about the morale of the East Enders is quite true.[32]

The people here are really standing up to it marvellously because these lengthening nights are far from pleasant and they may have lost their houses and all their possessions. . . .[33]

And the political scientist and socialist intellectual Harold Laski wrote to an American acquaintance: 'The people are simply superb. I know now why Lincoln had his ultimate faith in them. They know all they suffer, yet they take it with a calm and a strength I dare not try to put into words.'[34]

These fragments are by no means unchallengeable evidence. After all, people who were really terrified probably did not write letters at all. But none the less, they are characteristic of a range of material which does suggest that, despite the Blitz, morale remained high.

As opinion polls showed, a substantial majority of the British people were in favour of reprisal raids being carried out on the Germans, even though there was a superstition that this would simply bring further retaliation on themselves. No doubt certain sections of the press played a part in whipping up this reaction, but on the whole its manifestation seems to represent a perfectly genuine and fully understandable gut feeling. It has been argued that the Government deliberately encouraged reprisal demands in order to justify the area bombing of Germany. In fact the authorities preferred the self-image wherein the British were portrayed as stoically heroic and solidly good-humoured, for ever pouring out soothing cups of tea and letting drop quiet witticisms. A series of Pathé Newsreel post-Blitz interviews in which the *vox populi* comes through strongly in favour of immediate and massive reprisals – 'wicked old bugger like 'e is', says one interviewee of Hitler – were never shown. They were too much at odds with the preferred image.

The diaries of middle-class and upper-class people – for example, that of Kingsley Martin, editor of the intellectual socialist weekly, the *New Statesman* – are full of statements expressing exaltation over the excitements of the Blitz.

Here are some other middle-class reactions:

We stood by the window, looking out. I felt quite stunned but not by fear, but by the fantastic beauty of the scene. . . . I had such a sense of elation as I had never felt before. . . .

What a wonderful night we had last night! I hate war – I hate any kind of waste . . . and yet I could not help the feeling of exhilaration. . . .

. . . peaceful citizens are acquiring a strength and self confidence which will probably stand them in good stead all their lives, from their proved ability to stand up to such an ordeal as London has provided during the last week ; there is a sort of exaltation in the air.[35]

The majority no doubt did not feel exaltation. A WVS worker, in May 1941, entered this fundamental truth in her diary: 'Fear. Paralysing physical fear. It grips you and you feel contaminated, unclean.'[36] Fear of being burned to death or buried alive, of being ripped apart by blast or cut to pieces by shrapnel, was only too understandable. 'Tibby' Clarke, the famous Ealing Studios screenwriter, gives a thoroughly downbeat record of his experiences as a Special Constable: 'Of the blitz I shall write little. Most of us who went through it have ever since been wary of it as a subject lest we be labelled bomb bores. We in "S" Division were luckier than many London police, but we still had our fill of its cruelty and horror, its sickening destructiveness, its white dusty filth and its peculiar stink of fresh decay. . . . Just these few words and it begins to depress me again.'[37]

Yet throughout the nation psychological disorders (and suicides) declined, and there was no abnormal absenteeism. Throughout the country, shop-girls, typists and everybody else carried on in temporary premises or out-of-doors. *Plate 58* is rather set-up, yet it contains a real truth. Another way of demonstrating high morale was to contribute to War Weapons' Weeks (*Plate 60*).

Looting on a small scale was fairly widespread after air-raids, though there seems to have been a general disposition to excuse this on the grounds that otherwise the goods taken would have been lost anyway, or that they were some kind of reward for dangerous rescue work undertaken. Although the penalties referred to in *Plate 61* were never inflicted, the prevalence of petty looting is made clear by the fact that the maximum penalty on summary conviction was increased from

58   Girl clerks, temporarily forced to leave their London office as a result of enemy air-raids, carry on with the job in the open air. Steel helmets are their temporary 'roof', 17 October 1940.

59   *News Chronicle* photograph, 17 October 1940. The caption read: 'A hope realised: When this shop was bombed an optimistic management hoped that business would be almost as usual the next day. A *News Chronicle* photographer returned at the end of 24 hours and made his second picture. An outside scene of the shop as it is today'.

YOUR CITY STRIKES BACK
WITH £8,000,000

OAD CLO

60 Birmingham in 1940. War Weapons' Week.

six months imprisonment to one year. Curiosity about the effects of raids was another characteristic, people often coming some distance to view the results of a previous night's raid – some times to the extent of interfering with rescue and clearing-up work.

As a winter of bombs gave way to a spring of more bombs, the invasion fears of the previous summer revived. It was not known with certainty that Hitler had recognized, with his failure to gain air supremacy in the Battle of Britain, that his invasion plan (Operation Sea Lion) must be indefinitely postponed – in effect, abandoned. To many in high places April truly appeared the cruellest month, in which the risk of invasion stood at its highest. Again, as can be seen from the files of the Lord President's Office, there was much to-ing and fro-ing over the exact nature the counter-invasion plans should take. Some members of the House of Commons, on 12 February, had viewed the prospect of invasion with a touch of hilarity, but finally on 13 March 1941 the War Cabinet approved the issue of a further leaflet, 'Beating the Invader', which was issued to all householders in April. A second edition of this leaflet was held in readiness should there be a further definite warning that an invasion was imminent. It was not expected that anti-invasion plans would reach their highest state of efficiency till 1 September 1941; by August, the Government had in fact admitted that there was now little likelihood of an invasion actually taking place.

As far as overall morale is concerned, the picture is a mixed one – life (and, therefore, history) is like that. The myth-makers, the propagandists, the photographers, the cameramen, the editors, the

61 Warning to looters, 1940. The draconian punishments were never inflicted, but looting itself was common.

62 Guarding stock salvaged from a grocer's shop, Birkenhead, 15 March 1941.

journalists: all those responsible for creating images and stereotypes added much of the colouring. But even if the photographers employed the greatest professional skill in their representations of the Prime Minister, Churchill was real enough. The British people were real too. Not universal heroes, but ordinary human beings whose well-attested reactions to the dangers and rigours of total war provide a genuine basis for the stereotypes.

5 Evacuation (Again!) and Voluntary Service

The onset of the Blitz reactivated the evacuation movement. Whether evacuation in sum is to be seen as a social experiment which in the long run had beneficial consequences, or whether it is to be seen as a profoundly disturbing experience for the children involved, is still a matter of controversy. In many cases (though not in all: see *Plate 63*) the second evacuation took place in small numbers, rather than in the mass groups of September 1939, and it has been argued that this was an even more upsetting experience for the children involved than the earlier evacuation had been.

As had happened nine months previously, many of the deep social divisions within British society once more were sharply exposed. Householders were again disgusted by the habits of the slum children billeted on them; many attempted to evade their responsibilities for providing accommodation. Yet the hard evidence is that, although inevitably there were many personal frictions and problems of adjustment, on the whole relationships between hosts and billetees were much better, and characterized by greater sympathy and understanding, than they had been in September 1939. Naturally it wasn't all a story of social mixing: we read too of well-bred young ladies teaching horse-riding to evacuated prep schools.

Altogether, at the height of the second government scheme, 1,340,000 people were evacuated. By 1942 almost half of these had drifted home again; the worst of the Blitz was over, though, as we shall see, there were still to be many terrifying raids. Ultimately, the significance of the evacuation experience was that it brought to middle- and upper-class households a consciousness for the first time of the deplorable conditions endemic in the rookeries and warrens which still existed in Britain's great industrial cities, and so, among the articulate few, aroused a new sense of social concern. In this sense evacuation was a unique experience and one of the most significant phenomena of the war.

Still, it would be wrong to lay exclusive emphasis on evacuation. It was part of a wider movement in which middle- and upper-class people, voluntarily, or involuntarily, were projected into situations in which they were forced to accommodate themselves to some of the most appalling aspects of life as lived by Britain's poor. At the centre of this movement was the Women's Volunteer Service. In origins the

63 Children, leaving London on the fifth day of 'the great six-day evacuation', pass a detachment of troops at the railway station, 17 June 1940.

64 Evacuees shopping in Liskeard. The children in this photograph, published in *Illustrated* on 13 October 1941, are reassuringly well dressed. However, the picture is not misleading in conveying the generally better spirit informing the whole evacuation question by this time. The notices in the shop window provide some interesting further wartime detail.

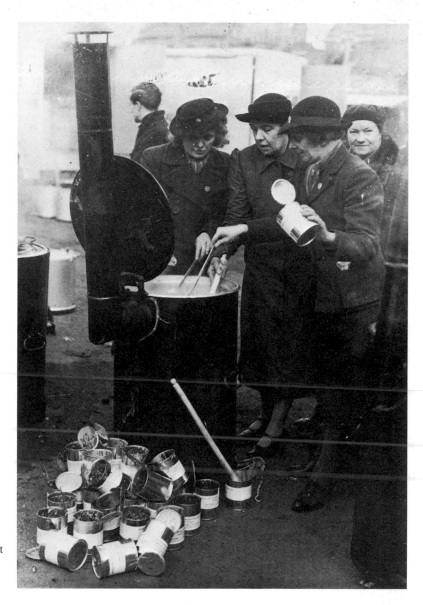

65 Members of the Women's Voluntary Service preparing hot food after the arrival of a food convoy at Coventry, 12 April 1941.

WVS was very much a product of the upper-class establishment of the 1930s: it was founded by Lady Reading with the informal support and approval of the Government. But perhaps women are less bound by class attitudes than men, or perhaps they are better able to exploit such attitudes for constructive purposes. In any event the WVS was an enormous success in canalizing the energies of middle- and upper-class women into the manifold urgent tasks of the Home Front. While it may be noted that the WVS organizer in Coventry was a Labour Councillor, Mrs Pearl Hyde, daughter of a publican, we also have to record the reflections of a middle-class woman holidaying late in the war at Wendover: 'I am quite enjoying my holiday. I go some mornings and sort paper for the WVS. I feel I ought to do something. One feels rather like a scavenger. I am getting to know Wendover's "best" people. I help a Lady Something.'

An early Mass Observation report (September 1940) remarked that the WVS 'is one of those curious hybrid official-voluntary organisations that are commonly supposed peculiarly the product of the Anglo Saxon genius'. As the same report puts it, the WVS 'acts as a kind of maid-of-all work to the established authorities'.

The Stepney branch of the WVS has only been formed within the past few months, but in the present emergency it has been doing excellent auxiliary work, providing helpers for the municipal authorities for evacuating the homeless and other tasks, assisting with transport, and operating mobile canteens for ARP, AFS [Auxiliary Fire Service] and other war workers. For example, when the investigator visited the people's palace on Saturday afternoon, September 21, he was told that the WVS had taken over from the municipal officials, who had gone home at 1 p.m., and had evacuated two hundred people.[38]

Quite certainly the 'women in green' were at least as important as, and probably considerably more in evidence than, the Home Guard. Providing meals and drinks in the heat and confusion of the Blitz was their most obvious role, but they played their part too in auxiliary welfare services, and, as the war wore on, in the salvage and make-do-and-mend campaigns. *Plate 65* shows women of the WVS in the thick of it in the Coventry Blitz. The cans of concentrated stew, labelled 'Ministry of Food', make clear the partnership between these women and an official organ of government. *Plate 66* shows well how private contributions (from the Queen and from the United States) meshed with government organization through the Ministry of Food which in turn meshed with the WVS.

Working among the poor was nothing new to such prominent East End figures as Father Groser, whom we met previously as the organizer of the Stepney Tenants League; but now a wider range of people were brought in to work in the many permanent canteens which began to spring up.

Rich upper-class girls, particularly the younger ones in some of the volunteer corps, confined their war contacts to driving officers around (French ones were particularly popular), but ambulance and salvage work (*Plate 69*) often involved middle-class volunteers in the life of poorer people.

Some of the most important aspects of voluntary welfare work were not photographed at all. The war gave a tremendous boost to the whole idea of social service, and many individuals were drawn into such activities as welfare visiting and the provision of play centres, which continued long after the immediate crisis of 1940–41 was over. Again, the most significant effect was to bring to the attention of middle-class people the appalling conditions in which so many lived.

66 The food convoy, drawn up for dispersal over the city after its arrival in Coventry, 11 April 1941.

Here is a description by one social worker (who set up a play centre in Paddington and endeavoured to take a large number of families into her care) of the conditions in which one such family lived:

I was asked to come into their room. It was one of the biggest rooms in the front of the house. . . . In front of me stood a big bed, dirty and not yet made. Between the bed and myself, just opposite anybody who happened to enter the room, stood an enormous chamber pot half filled with human excrement. One could not fail to see it. . . .

For the rest the room was littered with household things. Laundry, clean and dirty, covered the floor; the few bits of furniture were buried under heaps of stuff, and the impression of disorder of many years standing was bewildering and produced a feeling of hopelessness. The woman did not seem at all embarrassed that I should see the state of her room, but gave me the impression of being rather proud that she and her family occupied the biggest room in the house.[39]

But only so much could be done by voluntary action, even voluntary action openly or tacitly supported by government. In some areas direct government initiatives were essential. To deal with the sudden influx of air-raid casualties the Government had to create a unified Emergency Hospital Scheme, providing free treatment, and overcoming the petty rivalries which had obstructed the efficient functioning of the different types of hospitals in pre-war days. Gradually the scope of the EHS was extended, so that by the end of the war it provided a solid basis on which a National Health Service could be built. The Government also took a direct hand in sponsoring what Churchill decided to call British

67 East End communal rest and feeding centre for bombed people: Father Groser lends a helping hand. *News Chronicle*, 9 October 1940.

68 Working people and refugees eating a meal in the dining room of a wartime kitchen at Westbourne Terrace, Paddington, 5 March 1941.

69 Ambulance girls and salvage workers, amidst bomb damage, London. *Illustrated,* February 1941.

Restaurants, which provided a healthy, if unexciting, level of diet at very low cost (*Plate 76*). Among the many unlikely settings for the democracy of eating was the exclusive Pitt Club in Cambridge.

Although the photographer had probably carefully prepared the ground in advance, *Plate 12*, dating from December 1939, makes clear how much evacuated children welcomed a visit from their parents. In the second evacuation the Government made a conscious effort to provide cheap travel facilities for relatives to visit evacuees, but there were many anomalies, as this rather sad letter to the Minister of Transport makes clear:

Dear Sir, I hope you will excuse me if I am intruding by writing to you as I know you are a busy gentleman, but what I would like to know is why parents and friends of evacuees in Wales can have cheap fares to see their dear ones, yet there is no cheap fares for us to see our dear ones evacuated to Somerset. It is 10/8 from Soton [sic] to Hensbrady and Templecoombe. We cannot afford it. We are longing to see our child but cannot afford it. We have all her winter clothes ready and if they run cheap trains would kill two birds with one stone as the postal is dear, and if the fare was say a halfpenny a mile we could see the children as well as taking her warm clothes. Not only that, she would love to see us as she is only seven years old like hundreds of others get home-sick when they haven't got anything to look forward to seeing them. We haven't got cars to go and see them as the Directors of the Railways got. So they want to bear in mind that our children are as valuable and dear to us as any of the rich people's children. So I hope Sir this letter won't be delayed or falling on deaf ears till the rough cold weather sets in. Thanking you Sir to wake the railway officials up. I am, Sir, faithfully. . . .[40]

Householders in the reception areas seem to have been fairly tolerant of the frequent invasions on the part of parents and relatives, though as problems of local transport got worse and worse they tended not unnaturally to begin to protest about this.

CHAPTER FOUR

Austerity: 1941–43

1 Rationing and Queues

The second half of 1940 and the first half of 1941 were dominated by aerial attacks and threats of invasion. The following couple of months was dominated by the Battle of the Atlantic, the desperate fight to keep Britain's vital supply lines open in face of the depredations of German submarines. This was a period of austerity and tedium, interspersed by the occasional, but frequently quite devastating, air-raid.

Whereas in the previous world-conflict rationing had not been introduced till the very last year of the war, the Chamberlain Government managed to get round to it by January 1940, when, however, the bacon ration was actually fixed at a level higher than average pre-war consumption. In 1941, as the supply situation deteriorated, rations were curtailed. By mid-1941 some weekly rations amounted to no more than what in a respectable pre-war household would have been thought sufficient for a single helping: a shilling's worth of meat (about eight ounces), one ounce of cheese, four ounces of bacon or ham, eight ounces of fats (including not more than two ounces of butter), two ounces of jam or marmalade.

The Ministry of Food provided recipes for all sorts of strange substitute dishes: Woolton Pie (principally vegetables and potatoes), Lentil Roast, Carrot Tart – the latter glazed with lemon jelly to make a pudding. Apart from the basic rations, other foods were put on 'points', which allowed for a certain limited choice. For the privileged few, lavish meals were still obtainable in such places as Claridges, but, in general, eating habits were levelled out and institutionalized. Almost everyone – wealthy professional economist or Welsh coal miner who might well have been unemployed and on the poverty line before the war – was now eating at the level of the prosperous artisan of the inter-war years. The plain loaf of bread was very much in evidence as the staff of life for all classes (*Plates 70 and 71*).

On the whole, rationing was efficient and equitable, though there could be sudden shortages, particularly of fuel (*Plate 72*). There was monotony, indubitably, though some housewives no doubt enjoyed the challenge involved in, say, producing iced cakes without icing sugar, or banana sandwiches with parsnips and banana essence. Even for rationed goods to which you were entitled, there were usually

72 Paraffin shortage in Norfolk, 1941. 'Owing to a shortage of paraffin, families living in villages around Swaffham, Norfolk, have been without light for weeks, there is no gas or electricity supply, and candles are practically unobtainable.' *Illustrated*, 1941.

Opposite:
70 Evan Roderick Jones, a coal miner at Blainant Mine, Crynant, Glamorgan, at home with his family having Sunday dinner. *Illustrated*, September 1941. This meal would have consumed most of the week's meat supply, but it was certainly as good a meal as most miners would have had during the depression. Note that as well as bread there are plenty of potatoes on which to fill up; in keeping with the exhortations from the Ministry of Food the potatoes have obviously been scrubbed, not peeled, thus both avoiding waste and providing a more nutritious dish.

71 Sir Walter Layton, the economist, at home in Sussex, 1942. *Illustrated*, 8 September 1942. It is not possible to see what is being eaten, but the bread is a prominent feature.

queues. For anything particularly scarce, or subject only to irregular availability, there were always queues, sometimes of daunting length (though people seemed to have been resigned rather than daunted). Eggs were particularly prized (*Plate 73*).

Children grew up without ever having seen an orange (the wartime film *Millions Like Us* had a mock-factual caption describing this strange spherical object), let alone such exotica as pineapples. Food subsidies and price controls meant that the cost of living was kept down relative to wage increases. But that could be of little consolation when such highly prized items as cakes and confectionery were not available at all or, in making a rare appearance, had given rise to the usual instant, and enormous, queue (*Plate 75*).

Often, the best meals were to be obtained in the factory canteens or in the British Restaurants. A government social survey asked people: 'Do you consider the food you are getting at the moment enough to keep you fit?' Of male workers in heavy industry 58·3 per cent said 'yes', 41·7 said 'no'; of male workers in light industry 55·2 said 'yes', 44·8 said 'no'; of female workers in light industry 67·8 per cent said 'yes', and 32·2 said 'no'; as many as 78 per cent of housewives said that, as far as they were concerned, they were getting enough to eat, and 68·9 per cent thought that their children were getting enough to eat. Women

73 Queues, 1941. 'People in a London suburb queuing up for that all too rare egg at a farm supply shop.' 28 February 1941.

74 Empty shop in London, August 1942. Liquorice Allsorts seem to be the only item for sale in this confectionery shop. Note the list of maximum prices in the background. The notice on the right reads: 'Strict instructions have been given to the staff that in fairness to the general public no goods of any description are to be reserved for any customer.' Whether the detail was observed fully or not, the principle of equality and fair shares for all was being publicly paraded.

Opposite:
75 Queue for cakes outside the Carlton Cafe, Tonbridge, 1943.

76 British Restaurant, Gillingham, Kent, August 1941. The scene shows school-girls who act as waitresses. *Illustrated*, August 1941. One of the social evils of the First World War had been the way in which school-children were taken away from school to work 'in the national effort'. Great attempts were made in the Second World War to make sure that work such as this did not distract from a pupil's studies, but the picture can be taken as a fair representation of one aspect of the entire nation pulling together in the war effort.

77 Choosing a suit in wartime, May 1941.

were asked about the difficulties they were having with their shopping. Surprisingly, only 16·1 per cent claimed to be having difficulty, while 73·7 per cent said they were having no difficulty. Things were apparently tougher in Scotland (22·9 per cent having difficulty) and the north of England (24·6 per cent having difficulty).

The beauty of the points system was that, if the customer was limited in the total amount of any one type of commodity that he might buy, he did have a certain limited freedom of choice within the points available. The points system was applied to clothing, meaning in effect that people were rationed to one complete outfit a year, although, particularly for women, there was a certain leeway in regard to choice of scarves and other accessories (*Plate 82*). A utility scheme was devised whereby clothing and furnishings were made to certain restricted specifications which saved on raw materials. For poorer households this could sometimes mean that goods of sound functional design took the place of the trash produced commercially before the war. But it could also mean an intensification of the greyness of life. Turn-ups were abolished from men's trousers, though many men attempted to circumvent this by buying a size too large and then having the turn-ups made at home. New furniture could only be obtained by those setting up home for the first time, or those who had been entirely bombed out.

Churchill had been opposed to clothes rationing, declaring that he would not agree to 'stripping the people to the buff', but – as happened

78 Five families set out to make allotments from a Chelsea bomb-site, June 1942. Seen here are the Patrick family, busy on the patch of ground they have cleared. *Illustrated*, 25 June 1942. Chelsea, like Hampstead, was in those days still a very socially mixed area. It suffered much more seriously from bombing than did Hampstead.

often enough – those ministers responsible for the Home Front who knew conditions there better than did the great war lord had got their way. Despite the occasional brilliant improvisation, the community as a whole sank to a common level of dowdiness.

2 Make-Do and Mend

The Government set out to make Britain as self-sufficient as possible. Farmers were encouraged to cut down on their livestock farming (which, as is now well known, produces food in a very uneconomic way), to plough up their pasture land and, most important of all, to bring into cultivation that 'marginal land' which had been so long neglected. With government help, British farming now suddenly leapt towards total mechanization; during the war there was a three-fold increase in the number of tractors in use.

Ordinary town-living citizens were asked to do their part. 'Dig for Victory' became one of the great slogans of the war period. Householders dug up their lawns, and turned over their flowerbeds, the better to produce vegetables. Even bomb-sites were pressed into use (*Plate 78*).

There were also great campaigns to utilize all possible salvage materials. In 1940 the railings round public and private gardens began to disappear. Not all the materials which the Government called in were really usable in the war effort; or, if usable, they cost a

79 Housewife being helped with her salvage. According to the caption in the Popperfoto Archives, the ubiquitous representative of the WVS was in fact a duchess. Precise date not known.

disproportionate amount of money and effort to convert. As Minister of Aircraft Production, Lord Beaverbrook called for the housewives' aluminium pots and pans. It was not in fact practicable to convert them into the aircraft he promised. No doubt, however, such campaigns were of considerable value from the point of view of domestic morale: they made people feel that they were contributing something directly to the military effort, and they concentrated people's minds on the need to save and to salvage and, indeed (to use yet another of the great phrases of the time), to 'make-do and mend'.

The public were requested to separate out the different types of salvage, and it was said that the patriotic housewife kept at least four separate containers: one for tins and other metal – allegedly for the construction of aeroplanes and tanks; one for paper and cardboard, which of course was recycled (as we would say today), though at the time people were told that it would specifically be used to make food containers for the troops or cases for rifles and shells; one for bones, to be turned into glue (for aeroplanes, people were told) or glycerine (for explosives, of course); and most important, and most practicable,

80 Chislehurst and Sidcup Children's Salvage Corps. *Illustrated*, 24 October 1941,

81 F. W. Pethick-Lawrence making jam at his home in Gomshall, Surrey. *Illustrated*, 30 January 1942. Pethick-Lawrence was a well-known, and widely respected, upper-class socialist. He had also been a strong supporter of the Woman's Suffrage Movement. Whether it was due to this, or simply to the pressures of war, that he is seen here in the traditionally feminine role of making jam, is impossible to say.

82 No-coupon tailoring: clothes were made of materials unpicked from those discarded. The customer brings one of her old dresses to the counter for remodelling. *Illustrated*, 1941.

edible waste for feeding pigs. All households, at the very least, then, would have, in addition to the old style dustbin, a 'pig's bin' and a sack for paper. Children in particular were encouraged to go out actively in search of salvage (*Plate 80*).

In many respects there was a return to the pursuits of pre-industrial society, to do-it-yourself and make-it-yourself, to dressmaking, to jam-making, and to the horticultural pursuits of the smallholder. With both butter and manufactured jam very tightly rationed, and with bread again occupying a central place in most people's diet, jam-making became quite an important domestic occupation (*Plate 81*). One difficulty, inevitably, was the shortage of jam jars. One bachelor schoolmaster offered his pupils his collection of empty jam jars in return for having some of them filled with homemade marmalade.

Undoubtedly, the war spread the embrace of equality far more widely than ever before, though it remained true that those with wealth and with contacts could most readily circumvent some of the restrictions of wartime. Those who could afford it could bring their old clothes in to have them remodelled by a professional designer (*Plate 82*). Yet those who could not afford it could still do their best at home.

3 The Other Invasions

Hitler's invasion never materialized. But many people in various parts of the country suffered (or welcomed) other sorts of invasion. Apart from the evacuated mothers and children, factory workers and professional people were deliberately dispersed to safer parts of the country in order that they could continue with their work. There was

83 Underground aircraft factory, 21 August 1943. This factory occupied an uncomplicated section of the Underground in the Greater London area. Factory workers can be seen on the escalator.

also an influx of Commonwealth soldiers, of Poles, of Free French and then of Americans.

The dispersal of factories to rural areas could mean the injection of an urban working-class element into a predominantly agricultural and perhaps slightly 'backward' area, often with disruptive consequences for the local community. But since a large proportion of factory workers were in fact younger women, the social impact was often as considerable for them as for the host community. Frequently the girls were housed in hostels associated with the newly built factories. For many of them, it was a first experience away from the restraints, and security, of home. That splendid wartime film, *Millions Like Us*, recaptures this experience very well.

Sleepy towns with such evocative names as Chelmsford, Malvern and Chippenham became centres of war industry; there were over 250 shadow factories in various parts of the country, and about 40 Royal Ordnance factories, most of them, however, sited in the former depressed industrial areas of the inter-war years. The new government factories came to establish a high standard in factory welfare and in industrial relations; but in many areas the basic problems were those of overcrowding and inadequate accommodation. When, in 1942, the Telecommunications Research Establishment (responsible for the development of radar) moved to Malvern with 1,000 employees, its superintendent noted:

The average citizen of Malvern clearly did not want us. . . . potential billetors fell ill with alarming regularity and the number of destitute aunts who were being given permanent homes in a few days time passed all bounds of reason. Some gave shelter on the understanding that billetees were in by ten o'clock at night while others gave it on the understanding that they stayed out, somewhere, until the same hour.[41]

For middle-class professional people, dispersion from London to the provinces could often involve a sense of personal deprivation, though most were probably prepared to admit that they were better off without bombs falling about their ears. Different departments of the BBC went to various parts of the country (but the nine o'clock news and certain key programmes continued to be broadcast from London – even during a direct hit on Broadcasting House), parts of the Ministry of Agriculture went to Lytham St Annes, Pensions and National Insurance went to Blackpool (*Plate 84*), the Intelligence activities carried on at Bletchley are now well known, and a number of large private firms also moved to the country (*Plate 85*).

One important consequence of the dispersion of professional people from London was to create a demand for entertainment of a rather higher cultural level than was general in the British provinces; on the whole, through other developments which we shall discuss shortly, the consequences were positive.

The countries of Continental Europe suffered the trauma of forcible invasion by foreign troops, which, for the female population, could, at worst, mean rape, and at best, sexual liaisons formed by women in order to protect their own loved ones or to curry favour with the conquerors – horizontal collaboration, as the French colourfully called it. In Britain it could only be said of the Allied troops of various nationalities, either that they took the place of British men already removed from the scene, or that they proved more charming or more exotic than their native competition. The Poles, in particular, became a legend for their combination of dashing charm and old-world courtesy. Many in fact married and settled down in the United Kingdom, especially in Scotland. One stock joke of the time was that a memorial should be erected to all those Scottish women who had fallen for the Poles.

The Americans, of course, injected yet another element into human relationships. They kept to their own bases, surrounded by their own high standards of affluence and the attributes of their own civilization, venturing forth to stun some, and arouse the envy and hostility of others, by their parade of relaxed abundance. Out of a small sample of 150, Mass Observation found 46 Britons to be pro-American, 36 to be unfavourable to them, 55 managed to entertain both contrary feelings simultaneously, and 13 were 'vague'. Their most disliked characteristic was said to be their boastfulness. One man, characteristic of those who held contradictory views about the Americans, found them a rather swell-headed, mixed-blooded race, grossly misinformed as to the true state of world events. He noted their excessively high standard of living, and commented on their 'fast living' and attendance at night-clubs. He reckoned that the average American did not give a damn for anyone, which he thought a good thing in some ways. On the average,

84 Civil servants working in the filled-in swimming pool at Blackpool. This ministry photograph marvellously captures the feel of wartime bureaucracy. Precise date not known.

85 Employees of the Hearts of Oak Benefit Society evacuated to Herstmonceux Castle in Sussex. Precise date not known.

86 A Canadian soldier with a
girl in a London park, 3 March
1941.

he felt, they lived a much happier and more carefree life than British people did. In fact, he concluded that the American way of life was good, indeed very good, in *most* ways. None the less, the most common phrase about the Americans remained: 'The trouble with the Americans is that they are over-paid, over-dressed, over-sexed and over here.'

As well as their candy, chewing gum and transatlantic manners, the Americans brought their colour problem. The army paper *Current Affairs* (5 December 1942) sought to deal with the matter as delicately as possible:

The attitude of the British people towards the coloured troops is important from many points of view. Of course, all Americans are welcome here, whatever their creed, national heritage or colour. They are our guests and allies and as their hosts we have certain responsibilities. One of the responsibilities of a host is to avoid embarrassing his guests – and that is one good reason for avoiding thoughtless talk about the Colour Problem. . . .

It may well be that occasional cases will occur which might arouse the resentment and even anger of British troops and civilians who witness them. On the other hand, it is obviously highly unsuitable for the British to try to interfere in those instances. The troubles in India and Jamaica, racial relations in South Africa and the neutrality of Eire, are examples of our own unsolved problems which exist even though many of us see little of them face to face in this country.

It can be seen therefore that any attempts to break down the various forms of social regulation accepted by the average American family, white or coloured, is not likely to achieve any good purpose, but on the contrary might well lead to trouble and even violence, especially where women are concerned.[42]

99

Black soldiers apart, probably the facet which most emphasized the position of the Americans as a foreign army was the rather sinister appearance of their patrolling military policemen (*Plate 91*).

4 Communications and Propaganda

Many Poles remained, but their impact was felt purely at a personal level; most Americans did not, but their impact was felt on the wider values of society. Even without this direct injection of Americanization, British society at war moved definitively within the domain of modern mass communications.

The British documentary film was born and shaped in the 1930s, almost exclusively by the hands of men of liberal or left-wing sympathies. In wartime the British Government sponsored information films and supported feature films, most of them made by the men who had come to the fore in the thirties. Cinemas did well as people turned their backs on the strains and tedium of war. Newsreel production was pooled under government supervision, and newsreels remained jauntily patriotic, generally right wing in tone. There is evidence that some people found them irritating, but in the main they seem to have reflected what was acceptable to cinema audiences at the time.

Occasionally, quite strong left-wing, or at least populist, elements are apparent in wartime films. John Baxter's film of Walter Greenwood's famous novel of the depression, *Love on the Dole*, had been completed before war broke out, but so critical was it, by implication, of 1930s society, that it was not then released; when it was shown in 1940 it concluded with a brief message from the leading Labour Party figure A. V. Alexander (First Lord of the Admiralty in Churchill's Government) invoking a better future for the British people after the war. Baxter's *The Shipbuilders* (1943) was also remarkable for its authentic portrayal of the Glasgow working class from the inside, and contrasted remarkably with the view from above given in George Blake's original novel of 1935: again, for those with eyes to see, the message was of the imperfections of private enterprise. However, this sort of socialism merged easily into a generalized patriotism. The top moneymaker for 1942 was *The 49th Parallel*, a fairly 'hard' war film about German agents in North America. The top moneymaker for 1944 was the highly patriotic *This Happy Breed*. Even the, as it certainly now seems, excruciating Hollywood weepie *Mrs Minniver* seems to have gone down quite well with wartime audiences.

The drama of war created a craving for hard news, which the truncated newspapers, operating in the difficult conditions of wartime, could not satisfy. Sound broadcasting entered into its own because it could bring directly into the home or the air-raid shelter, not just the news bulletins but a number of other audio experiences directly associated with the war. There were the great exhortatory set-pieces

90 'Coloured People's Club: this club is open to "blacks" and "whites" and the poster is to remind visitors what happens if they practise a colour bar.' *Illustrated*, February 1943.

91 American military police in
a West End street, 1943.

92 Tommy Handley (right) seen at the microphone with Clarence Wright during an ITMA Broadcast from Bangor, May 1942.

93 Buying Defence Bonds in a Birmingham post office and general store, 1940. *Illustrated*.

from Churchill; there were homely talks from J. B. Priestley hinting at a better world after the war (though there was much opposition to him inside the Government); there was the Brains Trust, which catered for the need for serious discussion of serious topics; there were the various forms of light entertainment, which achieved new levels of sophistication and of popularity. Vera Lynn, 'The Forces Sweetheart', appealed to domestic audiences as well; Workers' Playtime was primarily part of the changing factory atmosphere, but could be listened to at home; Tommy Handley and ITMA ('It's That Man Again') reached great heights as a programme which was funny and topical, and introduced a fascinating range of characters only slightly larger than life (*Plate 92*). Many of the serious talks were undoubtedly pompous and patronizing, but the BBC did manage to develop a slightly lighter touch as the war wore on.

Much has been written, and continues to be written, about how in war 'truth' is 'the first casualty' – as if in peacetime governments and the mass media propagate nothing but 'truth'. Certainly, in a modern total war all means of communication had necessarily to be brought within government control. The Ministry of Information, set up at the beginning of the war, was in the early stages often dilatory, hesitant and downright contradictory in its policies. But the fact was that almost all newspaper proprietors, journalists, photographers and film-makers were only too anxious to follow the patriotic line. Gradually the Ministry of Information assumed a more authoritative position and established a good working relationship with the press, though, no doubt, as is the way with human institutions, it continued to make many foolish mistakes. On one occasion, a special news bulletin was released to the town of Hull, then withdrawn again on complaints being made that, if released to one town, it ought to be generally released.

Actually, censorship was indirect rather than direct. For major issues, the media in any case were dependent on the military authorities and the Government for their information. The Ministry of Information conducted briefing sessions in which 'guidance' was offered as to what line the press should take on particular issues. There was no advance censorship, but newspapers could of course be prosecuted or suppressed if they did print something which the Government thought they should not have done. In practice, the press submitted in advance all articles and photographs which it feared might be held to be against the patriotic interest. As we have seen in connection with evacuation, many newspapers continued to take an extremely right-wing line; however, the *Daily Mirror*, which had established a new image for itself in the 1930s, now rose to eminence as the paper which was, or at least claimed to be, determined to support the interests and aspirations of the ordinary people. *Picture Post*, another product of the thirties, was also very successful with its combination of what purported to be actuality photographs and radical journalism. Arguably, as my choice

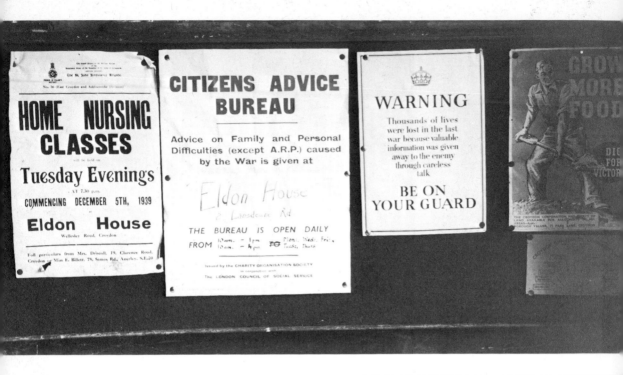

94 Posters in London (Croydon, in fact, as can be seen from the picture itself), 1940.

95 London Transport buses at Sidcup Garage, exact date uncertain. Plastered on the front of the first two buses is one of the most famous, or notorious, of all the wartime slogans. The buses are already showing some of the wear and tear of war, but the children look pretty spirited.

96 'Save Fuel' exhibition at Bethnal Green, London, 1943.

of illustrations for this book suggests, the photographs, if not the journalism, were better in its main rival, *Illustrated*.

Yet one of the most important forms of mass communication from the point of view of government propaganda remained the good old-fashioned poster. Neither posters nor photographs, neither newspapers nor films, had to be enlisted to propagate atrocity stories about the Germans. Everyone had had a bellyful of that in the First World War; and the irony was that when the first news of the German extermination camps began to filter through, editors refused to print them, believing them to be mere propaganda. Posters were used instead for exhortation, guidance and advice on such matters as war savings (*Plate 93*) digging for victory or saving fuel (*Plates 94, 96 and 99*).

Just to see a selection of posters, together with their surrounding environment, is to learn an enormous amount about the Home Front. *Plate 93* shows a beautiful 1930s-style shop, with a wonderfully miscellaneous range of goods and interesting peacetime commercial advertising. Presumably, the picture of Queen Mary had been there since before the death of her husband, George V, in 1937. Soon the notion of 'Defence Bonds' gave place to the simpler phrase 'War Savings', and many of the slogans became rather more memorable than the one shown in the shop. The idea of war savings-stamps had been pioneered in the First World War and was a very democratic one, opening the opportunity of savings to (and of course, from the

Government's point of view, tapping the potential of) people with low
incomes.

Recently, Tom Harrisson has seized on the slogan:

YOUR COURAGE

YOUR CHEERFULNESS

YOUR RESOLUTION

WILL BRING

US VICTORY

to demonstrate the arrogant establishment view that the people will
make the effort, but it will be us, the establishment, who will achieve
victory. Certainly, there is plenty of documentary evidence of this sort
of attitude at the Ministry of Information and elsewhere in the
Government. At the same time, Sir John Reith, first Director-General
of the BBC and briefly Minister of Information at the beginning of the
war, had, in February 1940, laid down as a first 'Principle and
Objective of British Wartime Propaganda', the statement that, 'This is
your war, the nation's war.' Thus the slogan can legitimately be read in
a different sense: 'you', the people, are being appealed to, and the basic

concept seems to be of government and people together, 'us', being involved in victory.

Such an interpretation, stressing *participation*, seems to be borne out by some of the other posters. The war gave an enormous boost to Citizens' Advice Bureaux, where citizens could get advice as to their rights against the authorities. It is true that there was quite a strong element of private charity behind the sponsorship, as we can see in *Plate 94*, where the Bureau poster was issued 'by the Charity Organisation Society in conjunction with the London Council of Social Service'.

But participation does seem to be a keynote in *Plate 96*: this is 'Bethnal Green's own Domestic Front exhibition'. Note particularly the poster about the Ministry of Food Advice Service. In *Plate 97*, we see an advertisement for one of the most beneficial schemes connected with the war effort, the scheme which enabled thousands of men and women to have their skills up-graded. *Plate 98*, of course, takes us back to a more traditional type of propaganda, though the rather neat slogan, 'Tanners for Spanners', is worth a moment's attention, as is the caricature of Hitler receiving the blast of a shell in his face.

Plate 99 gives a nice range of different types of poster, including the two commercial ones for Black and White whisky and Marshall's table foods. Shank's Pony (far left) was another great wartime rediscovery: going on foot was a necessity both to conserve scarce fuel and spare transport for essential war purposes, and because wartime transport was so awful anyway. On the far right, the military target imagery is rather well done. Recruitment of women is an obvious subject, and 'dig for victory' and 'war savings' we have met before. One slogan not quoted in any of this entire range of posters is 'careless talk costs lives', though there is a direct presentation of this theme (obviously the slogan had not been coined yet) in *Plate 94*.

100   Bomb damage at Exeter. This photograph was not taken till October 1943, though the raids took place on 24 April and 3 May 1942. The picture gives a good impression of the longer-term effects of bomb-attacks, and shows the tradesmen's boards with their new addresses.

101   'Ancient city of Bath raided: the ancient city of Bath was recently attacked by German bombers in their "Baedeker" raids. In this picture, just released, can be seen the damaged Regina hotel and assembly hall (right).' Passed by the censor, but with the note: 'must not be published before the morning papers of Tuesday, May 26th [1942]'. The raid had actually taken place a month earlier.

5 The Baedeker Raids

The most serious threat facing Britain in this period was the increasing toll exacted by German submarines: the tonnage lost in the North Atlantic in the first six months of 1942 was almost a million greater than in the comparable period in 1941. Anxious to carry the war direct to Germany, and entertaining exaggerated notions of the destructive effect mass bomb-attacks would have on German civilian morale, the British Government began a new phase of 'strategic bombing' of German cities. Hitler's response was, on 14 April 1942, to order the 'Baedeker Raids' (so-called after the famous German Baedeker guidebooks) on British cities of outstanding historical value and beauty.

The period of the intensive Blitz had forced people, particularly in London and the south-east, to adopt a completely new pattern of life, in which nightly bombing had to be accepted as part of the norm. After the summer of 1941 something more like the old routine could be

resumed, though of course there were all the other disruptions and irritations of war, and there was no way that bomb damage could suddenly be made good. It is also important to remember that here and there quite devastating raids took place between the end of the sustained Blitz and the Baedeker phase, and these continued into 1943.

The Baedeker attacks began on 24 April 1942 when Exeter was bombed for the first time (*Plate 100*). Bath came next, when two successive night-raids resulted in the deaths of 400 people (*Plate 101*). After York and Norwich had been raided, there was a second really devastating attack on Exeter on 3 May. A further attack on Norwich was unsuccessful, possibly because a balloon barrage had meantime been assembled, or perhaps because of the existence of a decoy site near the town (a device used several times with considerable effect during the war). Canterbury was attacked on 31 May, producing, as in earlier blitzes, the familiar picture of 'trekkers' (*Plate 105*). Canterbury was attacked again on 2 and 6 June; and the last Baedeker raid, again aimed at Norwich, took place towards the end of June. Because these towns were relatively small, and rather ill prepared, the raids were all quite serious and long-lasting in their effects (*Plate 100*).

Occasional daylight raids still had to be endured, even after the Baedeker series was formally concluded. One of the worst of these came on south-east London on 20 January 1943. A three-storey

102 Soldiers, Civil Defence workers and civilians clearing the debris while searching for survivors amid the ruins of the bomb-damaged school. Photograph dated 20 January 1943, and marked as 'banned'.

103 The crowd look on as the rescue work continues. Picture dated 21 January 1943 and marked as 'banned'. Such a picture was obviously regarded by the Censorship Bureau as bad for morale.

building which housed a primary school in its first two floors, and Catford Central School for Girls in the top floor, sustained a direct hit. The girls had been evacuated to Smarden and Charring in Kent in 1939, but in common with so many others had by this time returned to London. Thirty-eight children and six adults were killed. Although the newspapers printed some pictures of the bomb damage, the more harrowing photographic results (*Plates 102, 103 and 104*) were banned by the censor.

104 The bodies of some of the victims recovered from the bombed school. Picture dated 21 January 1943 and marked as 'banned'. Generally British photographers did not take pictures of dead bodies, even if wrapped in sacking as here. There was certainly a convention that such photographs were not published in the war.

105   Nazi raid on Canterbury: homeless people making their way through bombed streets, 2 June 1942. The attack had only taken place a few nights before on 31 May, but the picture is marked as passed by the censor.

Thus, although the worst of the Blitz was long since over, bombing did not totally cease in the summer of 1941. All of Britain's major cities continued to bear the scars and the serious inconveniences of the ordeals they had earlier suffered. The censor, however, continued to prefer pictures of cheerful, animal-loving Britons, carrying on regardless (*Plate 106*).

6 The Iconography of War

106   Feeding an injured cat among the debris of a bombed street in the London area, 20 January 1943.

For merchant seamen, life in the middle years of the war was still desperately perilous; for civilians, where there were no bomb-attacks, it was often simply tedious and irritating. Food rations were low, though sufficient for the maintenance of healthy existence, and cigarettes, sweets and beer were often quite unobtainable. The iconography of wartime Britain could often be deeply depressing: barrage balloons in the sky or, presenting rather a different aspect, moored to the ground (*Plate 109*); barbed wire and pill boxes at the beaches; some areas (such as those round bridges) totally closed; large areas of land taken over by ugly military establishments; everywhere the evidence of raids and invasion scares; derelict sites, place-names still missing, shops boarded up (*Plate 107*).

All sorts of stories got about as to how the balloons functioned. Mass Observation reported one man as saying that the barrage was electrified and drew aeroplanes like magnets, bombs being attracted by the cables and sliding harmlessly down them.

At various points on the coast the public were allowed access to the delights of a day on the beach. Around the barbed wire entanglements the military kept a watchful eye on visitors to see that they did not stray.

The grumbling of those who had enjoyed private motoring before the war intensified. But then only about 30 per cent of the male population had ever held a driving licence, and a third of them had only had experience of driving commercial vehicles. What held greater significance was the growing number of people (34 per cent in the

107 Sturry Post Office: the name was painted out, and there was nothing to put in the windows except black-out material and posters issued by the Government.

108 Wreckage dump in Hyde Park: baths salvaged from bombed homes. *News Chronicle* photograph passed for publication, 20 March 1941.

109 Grounded barrage balloon.
No precise date known.

Government's own *Social Survey* of September 1943) dissatisfied with the public transport facilities for getting to and from work. At times, too, certain bits of war news, above all the fall of Singapore in 1942, had a particularly depressing effect on civilian morale.

Yet, though it would be dangerous to take at face value the nostalgia of those who now look back to the Second World War as the time when the nation had a true sense of purpose and when everyone cheerfully pulled together, it is important to remember that for many even the dullest period of the war was a time of exhilaration and purposefulness; certainly, most people, one way or another, managed to go on enjoying life.

Ballroom dancing, whether with a chosen life partner or with a complete stranger (and wartime was full of complete strangers), reached a peak of popularity, often accompanied by the sentimental melodies sung by Vera Lynn, and sometimes in very unpropitious circumstances, far from a ballroom (*Plate 111*).

There was money about, and even some of those who in pre-war days would never have dreamed of eating in a restaurant, joined in the search for the fashionable little places which somehow managed to supply fairly reasonable meals. Such a place was Mrs Staines's restaurant in Chilworth Mews (*Plates 112 and 113*). Much in evidence are uniforms, both military and civilian, on men and women. Earlier in the war the censor had been slow to stop newspaper pictures of wealthy people eating expensive meals (*Plate 53*); now, however, the censorship saw fit to suppress pictures of these perhaps slightly un-British scenes of people enjoying eating and drinking together, and even sitting outside in Continental style.

There were places where traditional seaside activities could be enjoyed unhampered by barbed wire; only the soldiers in uniform showed that there was a war on (*Plate 114*).

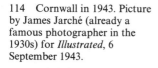

114   Cornwall in 1943. Picture by James Jarché (already a famous photographer in the 1930s) for *Illustrated*, 6 September 1943.

CHAPTER FIVE

Social Change: 1942–45

1 Labour, Politics and Social Security

The existence of irritation and war weariness was clearly shown in the steady growth of industrial strife. The number of days lost due to strikes rose throughout 1942, 1943 and 1944, dropping slightly in 1945, when it was still double what it had been in 1939. But this militancy also reflected the consciousness of the working class of its strong bargaining position: government and indeed employers preferred to concede higher wages, rather than risk a serious disruption to the national war effort, or to the high profits to be made in the war industries.

The strength brought to the Labour movement by the war can be seen in a number of ways. The major Labour Party leaders were in the Government, and the most important trade-union figure of all, Ernest Bevin (*Plate 57*), was close to Churchill, though, it will be recalled, he had never, prior to 1940, been in Parliament. Labour played a leading part in the various moves towards developing reconstruction policies for the post-war era.

Since Conservatives, Labour (and Liberals) were bound together in the same national coalition, opposition to the Government at by-elections, in favour, say, of more support for Soviet Russia or of more vigorous social policies, could only come from organizations outside the three major parties. A number of upper-class Liberal intellectuals founded Common Wealth which succeeded in winning several by-elections; then there were the smaller socialist parties, such as the ILP (Independent Labour Party) and the Socialist Party of Great Britain. The Scottish Nationalists did well, making a particular issue of the transfer of Scottish girls to England to work in munitions factories under, it was alleged, highly immoral conditions. Opposed to the war, and subject to highly suspicious scrutiny by the Government, up till the time of the German invasion of Russia (the Communist paper, the *Daily Worker*, was banned for eighteen months from 21 January 1941), the Communist Party was now an enthusiastic supporter of Allied victory.

Thus one of the most fascinating by-elections of all took place in April 1942, after Churchill had decided to convert his friend Sir James Grigg, Permanent Under-Secretary at the War Office, from a civil servant into a full-time politician and statesman. A seat in Parliament had to be found for Grigg, and to the people of Cardiff East there fell the signal honour of providing this. In a highly diverting by-election campaign Grigg, a vehement supporter of private enterprise, had the vociferous support of the Communist Party, as well as the Government parties, but faced the opposition of Fenner Brockway of the ILP, complete with female bill posters (*Plate 115*). The local press reported:

At a meeting at the Splott-Road Schools, organised by the Splott Ward of the Labour Party in support of Sir James Grigg, Mr. Idris Cox, Communist, welcomed the opportunity of cooperating with the Labour Party in the by-election, and emphasised that the real issue was 'For or Against Fascism'. Whatever differences existed on other matters, there should be no doubt on the need for national unity against the common enemy of mankind.

The Communists have always fought for 'Socialism', he said, 'but the ILP simply indulges in empty phrases about "Socialism now," while their actual policy has helped Fascism ever since Mussolini's invasion of Abyssinia and the ILP leaders have always attacked Russia.'

It was the duty of the electors to vote for Sir James Grigg.

Cat-Calls at ILP Meeting
Such was the barrage of questions, interruptions, and cat-calls at Saturday night's rally of the ILP at the Cory-hall that at times the speakers were unable to proceed. Members of the audience in various parts of the hall shouted at each other, and terms of abuse were plentiful, particularly between supporters of the Communist Party and those of the ILP.

Speakers on the platform were Mr. Fenner Brockway (candidate), Mr. James Maxton, M.P., and Mr. John McNair (general secretary of the ILP).

We should take that newspaper account, with its total patriotic support for the cause of Sir James Grigg, with a slight pinch of salt. Undoubtedly, a strong radical opinion, which was often dissatisfied with the official government position, and the support which the Labour Party had to give to it, was building up. While the Communists had presented themselves as loyal supporters of Grigg, they, naturally, took a lead in trying to press the Government to give still more aid to Soviet Russia, and in particular to take the pressure off Russia by opening an immediate second front in Europe (*Plate 116*). Russia was widely popular, and many of those whose own aspirations were towards greater social equality in Britain saw her as a symbol of what they themselves were striving for.

Public opinion was again aroused when Britain's leading Fascist, Sir Oswald Mosley, who had been imprisoned at the beginning of the war, was released towards the end of 1943. The prominent part played by women in such political activities (*Plate 115*) may be noted; it is not surprising that 'equal pay for equal work' was one of the great political slogans of the later period of the war, coming as near as anything could to the cry for 'votes for women' which had marked the closing stages of the previous world war (*Plate 117*).

Outright opposition to the war was actually numerically stronger than it had been in 1914–18, though it never seemed to attract as much attention. On the whole, the legal provision for conscientious objection was much more scrupulously and sympathetically applied than it had been previously, when the tribunals of the Great War had made

115   Wartime by-election at Cardiff East. Sir James Grigg, War Minister, and Fenner Brockway, ILP, were the candidates. Male bill posters in Cardiff had evidently all joined up, so the women came into their own at the election. *Illustrated*, 10 April 1942.

TEA
SOLD HERE
END THE
WAR BY
VOTE FOR
Meeting
SMITH LECTURE THEATRE
CATHAYS PARK
20th MARCH
At 5.45 p.m.
World Traveller & Lecturer
DONALD GRANT
WILL SPEAK ON
"How Soviet Russia
Prepared for Hitler"
Esq., J.P., F.C.A
FREE

Opposite:
116 'Second Front Now'.
Harry Pollitt, outside the rear
entrance to the British Museum,
addresses a huge crowd on aid to
Russia, 1943.

117 Equal pay for equal work:
a meeting in progress in
Trafalgar Square, 4 June 1944.

118 The first female
conscientious objector was, it
seems, twenty-year-old Miss
Hilda Henshall-Brown of
Manchester, who refused to take
up nursing work when she
registered with her age group for
national service. Like her family,
she belonged to the Jehovah's
Witnesses. The regulations did
not provide for the situation and
'her case has puzzled officials.'
14 June 1941.

themselves notorious for their irrational and sadistic behaviour. However, it is scarcely surprising that little photographic evidence of male conscientious objectors exists. Conscription of women posed the puzzling question of conscientious-objector status for them, which, in fact, was shortly granted (*Plate 118*).

It is clear from public-opinion surveys, government investigations and the private reports of Mass Observation, that people wanted there to be a better world after the war than the one they had known in the 1930s, though they were not in most cases very optimistic about getting it. But the very involvement in the war, both in the auxiliary services at home and in the armed forces, meant that people became better educated and more aware of themselves: they had, in today's jargon, 'heightened consciousness'. Many took to reading during the long spells in the shelters, particularly paperback Penguin books, which often had a left-wing political character. Much against the wishes of many Conservative members of the Government, the Army Bureau of Current Affairs, a wartime creation, fostered an interest in social and political questions. (Churchill's view, expressed to his War Secretary, was unequivocal – though, as often in such matters, it failed to carry the day: 'I hope you will wind up this business as quickly and decently as possible, and set the persons concerned to useful work.') The director of ABCA was associated both with Penguin Books and with the Workers Educational Association. One Tory at the War Office said of him: 'his life was so largely wrapped up in music and art that I doubted his capacity to keep the morale of the Army as a fighting force in the forefront.' And the same man said of ABCA that its 'whole tendency . . . is towards the soft life and total reliance on the State to provide everything from the womb to the tomb.'

Yet despite these reactionary views inside the War Office, many Conservative politicians, as well as leading industrialists, did accept that the war had made necessary new initiatives in social planning. Speaking of the Londoners' defiance in face of the Blitz, *British Industry*, the journal of the Federation of British Industries, declared, 'So great a people deserve the best. We must build again.' In the summer of 1941 the Conservative Post-War Problems Committee was founded by R. A. Butler, an intellectual and a patrician figure of liberal sentiments who had been chosen by Churchill as President of the Board of Education. In his autobiography Lord Butler has declared that, 'The crisis of modern war is a crucial test of National values and way of life. Amid the suffering and the sacrifice weaknesses of society are revealed and there begins a period of self-examination, self-criticism and movement for reform.'

William Temple, Archbishop of York until 1941, thereafter Archbishop of Canterbury, emerged as the most important non-political figure to support social reform. Sir Richard Acland, son of a distinguished Liberal MP, founded Common Wealth, which, though to begin with mainly an organization of intellectuals, gradually attracted rank-and-file Labour support frustrated by the wartime political truce. Common Wealth popularized the notion of 'a people's war *and* a people's peace'.

But it was because of direct pressure from the official TUC that an inter-departmental committee of civil servants under the chairmanship of Sir William Beveridge was appointed to 'undertake . . . a survey of the existing national schemes of social insurance and allied services . . . and to make recommendations'. Beginning life as a journalist, Beveridge had been associated as a civil servant with the Edwardian social-insurance reforms; he had been a top civil servant in the First World War, an academic administrator in the inter-war years and chairman of a number of important committees. Yet his new commission did not immediately please him (he was a very unpopular man, and it is probable that the Government wished to sidetrack him away from other work more obviously central to the war effort); as he wrote to his sister on 29 July 1941, 'I'm Chairman also of a Reconstruction Committee on the Social Services: but I'm not doing much about that while I can do anything about the war.'[43] It was fortunate that the Secretary to the committee, D. N. Chester, was a temporary wartime civil servant from a working-class background who had been a lecturer in Public Administration at Manchester University.

Strictly speaking, the deliberations of the Beveridge Committee should have been mainly confined to the technical aspects of social insurance. But all aspects of social policy were now a matter of general debate. Shortly after the members of the Beveridge Committee were appointed, the Minister of Health, Ernest Brown, referred in the House of Commons (9 October 1941) to future health policy: 'The question of post-war hospital policy and reorganization, more particularly in relation to the Emergency Hospital Scheme, has for some time been engaging the attention of the Government. . . . It is the objective of the Government as soon as may be after the war to ensure that by means of a comprehensive hospital service appropriate treatment shall be readily available to every person in need of it. . . .'[44] Brown nevertheless made it clear that the Government did not envisage a completely free hospital service. Replying to a Glasgow doctor in June 1942, Beveridge described health policy as falling 'about half in and half outside my terms of reference'.[45]

The bulk of the report was indeed concerned with the 'Social Insurance and Allied Services' of the terms of reference. The major innovations were that the insurance scheme should cover all classes in society, that it should cover all possible contingencies, and that it should provide uniform benefits which would guarantee minimum subsistence; as a good liberal, Beveridge believed that it should be left to the individual to make additional provision through private insurance. What transformed the report into a truly historic document was the insistence that, 'Organization of social insurance should be

119　Sir William Beveridge at work on his report, 1942.

treated as one part only of a comprehensive policy of social progress.' Simultaneously, the report declared, albeit in somewhat Victorian terminology, that there must be attacks on ill health, inadequate education, bad housing and unemployment. The successful implementation of his social security proposals, Beveridge insisted, depended on three assumptions: the institution of children's allowances, a comprehensive health service, and 'maintenance of employment, that is to say avoidance of mass unemployment'.

Even while it was being drafted the Beveridge report ran into all kinds of difficulties. The files of the Beveridge Papers in the London School of Economics reveal clearly the powerful attacks which were mounted by the vested interests of the insurance and medical professions, and also from within the Government itself. In his evidence to the Beveridge Committee, the Director of the Federation of British Industries expressed his hostility, though he said that he did not wish to make it public. He also unintentionally put his finger on the central irony of the war, that despite the views of him and his kind the war was bringing about social change: 'we did not start this war with Germany in order to improve our social services; the war was forced upon us by Germany and we entered it to preserve our freedom and to keep the Gestapo outside our houses, and that is what the war means.'[46] The moment the report was published the opposition was open and vociferous. There was much invocation of the British race and the British character, both of which, it was argued, would be destroyed by the Beveridge proposals. The Federation of British Industries now overtly dropped its former progressive stance of 1941, the *Daily Telegraph* was mainly hostile, and a leading figure in the insurance world declared that, 'If this scheme were to come to pass, truly might not Ribbentrop allege the Anglo-Saxon race was decadent.'

It is now fashionable to point out that much of the Beveridge report, as was probably inevitable, was aimed at remedying the abuses of the 1930s and certainly contained nothing very revolutionary. It is also said, quite inaccurately, that the report had the support of all political and professional opinion.

What the report does seem to have had is the support of the majority of the British people. Two weeks after publication, a national opinion poll found that 95 per cent of those interviewed showed some knowledge of the report; 88 per cent approved the idea of doctor and hospital services for all (showing how one of the 'assumptions' achieved central importance); 53 per cent believed the Government would put the plan into operation, while 18 per cent doubted this. A year later it was reported that 256,000 copies of the full report had been sold and 369,000 copies of an abridged version (a further 40,000 copies were sold in the United States).

Churchill was unenthusiastic about the Beveridge report, and it was not published until 2 December 1942; there was no parliamentary debate on it until 16 February 1943. While the Ministry of Information seized on the report as a powerful propaganda weapon, Sir James Grigg suppressed the attempt of ABCA to circulate a summary of its contents to the troops. In the parliamentary debate two government spokesmen, Sir Kingsley Wood and Oliver Lyttelton (both Conservatives), were so feeble and hesitant in their support of the Beveridge report that they aroused the justifiable suspicion that the Government had no serious intention of implementing it. From the records we can see the enormous efforts which were made by the Labour Party, particularly acting through its General Secretary J. S. Middleton, by Attlee who drafted a most pungent memorandum on the subject to Churchill, and by D. N. Chester to ensure that the Beveridge report would indeed be implemented. In fact, in 1943 and 1944 the Government issued a series of White Papers which committed it to the main lines of the Beveridge proposals and to a general policy of social planning and reform.

It is fairly easy to pin down the views of individuals on questions of social reform; when we try to generalize about public attitudes as a whole, then we are on much trickier ground. However, the work of Mass Observation, in particular, and of other opinion surveys, make some generalizations possible. It does seem that the main effects of the first three years of war were to make people less pre-occupied with themselves and their immediate problems than they had been in 1938; most thoughts, in fact, were concentrated on the war effort itself. Around the end of 1942 a further change becomes apparent. The Beveridge report, together with the controversies surrounding it, marked something of a watershed. It harmonized fully with the popular concern, formerly only vaguely formulated, but now becoming rather better articulated, with social security. Now people began to express themselves more firmly about their belief in social

120 The Prime Minister leaving a textile mill after a tour through the works, 17 December 1942

change, and they began to be more specific about the particular changes which they thought ought to be made.

Within this context, it is not surprising that there were grave doubts about Churchill's position as a potential post-war leader. Mass Observation surveys showed that, while Churchill's standing as a military leader was still very high, 62 per cent in 1944 thought that he would be a bad peacetime leader. Furthermore, there undoubtedly were pockets of hostility towards Churchill, motivated by a variety of grievances; yet it would be ludicrous to deny his unchallengeable stature as a great and popular war leader. At best, the evidence of *Plate 120* is a trifle ambiguous. Churchill himself often gave the victory sign in a manner identical to that of the vulgar V-sign popularly used, and this style was imitated recently by the present leader of the Conservative Party when celebrating a Tory by-election victory. There is perhaps a certain light-hearted mockery to be detected in the attitudes of those women who are out of Churchill's line of vision.

Even the hostile graffiti in public lavatories (described by a number of contemporaries) have their limitations as evidence of any real popular hostility to the wartime Prime Minister.

121 Women's Land Army: three of the girls working a tractor. *Illustrated*, 11 September 1939.

2 Women at War: The New Image

In the First World War it was only under great pressure and with great reluctance that government and employers conceded the necessity for extending employment opportunities to women. The breakthrough at last came with the introduction of conscription for men in 1916. In the Second World War we have seen how conscription was introduced from the very beginning, and the Government was forearmed with the knowledge of the crucial role women had played in the previous war.

Yet, much of the early organization of women's employment was marked by that upper-class amateurishness which had tinged the, in all important respects, efficient and successful WVS. The energetic Lady Reading was also invited just before the war to begin the organization of a Women's Land Army, in a simple repetition of a fairly successful innovation of the previous war. To begin with, the Women's Land Army had a rather debby or at least girls' school atmosphere, and it was fully in keeping with its establishment origins that no attempt was made at consultation, let alone joint action, with the agricultural trade unions. None the less, after this early start, the expansion of women's employment on the land was rapid, and in the end much greater and

122 November 1939. At work inside the office of the postal censorship departments in the north.

more successful use of women's labour was made than had ever been the case in the first war. In 1939, 93,000 women had been employed on the land; by June 1945 there were 204,000. Only a relatively small minority of these – 65,000 – were enrolled in the Women's Land Army.

By 1939 women were already prominent in clerical work; as early as 1929, partly as a consequence of the transformations of the previous war, 25 per cent of those employed in the non-industrial Civil Service were women. As *Plate 122* shows, most of the workers recruited for the new postal censorship departments were women: but this fact was not thought to be worthy of any special comment in the contemporary caption attached to the picture. Naturally, the Civil Service as a whole expanded greatly during the war period, but within that expansion there was a disproportionate growth in the employment of women. There had been 95,000 women in the non-industrial Civil Service in 1939; by October 1944 there were 320,000 women, 48 per cent of the total.

In other jobs, however, the growth of women's employment was not so immediately noticeable. Women had worked as bus and tram conductresses in the First World War, but had disappeared from that employment with the return to peace. Only in the crisis summer of 1940 was a return made to the experience of the previous war. As can be seen from *Plate 123*, initially the women had no uniforms. And, in fact, for the first two or three days they were supervised by men. But once started the expansion was rapid; soon it was unusual on any form of transport to see male ticket collectors.

Despite some evidence from the first war to demonstrate the contrary, it had been expected that, where women were substituted for men, in most industrial jobs it would require three women to do the work of two men. By 1941 women were being employed on heavy manual tasks (*Plates 124 and 125*).

Certainly modern technology made industrial employment for women more practicable, and already in the thirties the developing engineering, light-metal and electrical industries had provided new opportunities for them. The war greatly accelerated this particular trend. The number of women employed in engineering and vehicle building increased by 770,000, the proportion of women employed rising from 9 per cent to 34 per cent. In many ways the new glamour

123 'The first of London Transport's lady conductors starts off: lady conductors of the London Passenger Transport Board commenced their first duties very early this morning at Swanley Garage (country services).' 18 July 1940.

124 'Women recruited by the Islington Borough Council to clear raid debris fill sandbags and do other labouring tasks. They started off on three-quarters of the men's rate of pay.' 22 May 1941.

125 Women navvies building an aerodrome in East Anglia. *Illustrated*, 16 September 1941.

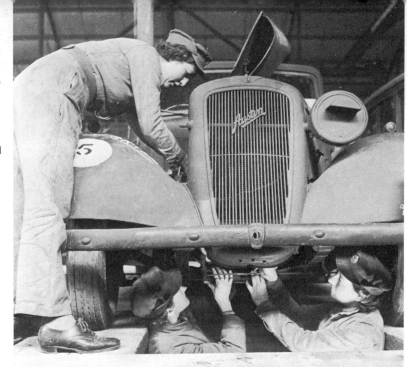

Opposite:

126 Woman factory worker on the body of a Spitfire, 1941.

127 Women's Home Defence Corps, September 1942. Girls practising small-arms firing, under the guidance of a corporal of the Home Guard.

128 ATS Motor Transport Depot: drivers Evans and Ashton working in the pits. *Illustrated*, June 1942.

129 Tank assembly shop in north-east England, March 1942.

employment for women, celebrated in novels and, above all, in films, was skilled work in the new aircraft factories (*Plate 126*).

Conscription of women was introduced in December 1941, though it was to play a very minor role in the changes in women's employment during the war. Married women not living apart from their husbands were wholly exempt, as were women with children under fourteen years of age. Of those not thus exempt only women of the age group nineteen to twenty-four were in practice called-up, whereupon they had the choice between serving in the auxiliary services (in which they would not be called upon to handle a lethal weapon unless they signified willingness to do so in writing), civil defence or certain specified forms of civilian employment. At the end of the war there were rather fewer than half a million women enrolled in the WRNS (Women's Royal Naval Service), the ATS (Auxiliary Territorial Service) and the WAAF, and the larger proportion of these were volunteers, not conscripts. However, as can be seen from *Plate 127*, the Home Guard idea was extended to women.

In many cases, the women who did go into military uniforms found themselves doing exactly the same sort of tasks as they would have been doing in peacetime: cooking meals or, at best, doing clerical work. Some women, it is true, had responsible roles to play in RAF control towers, and in anti-aircraft batteries; they also took on a range of other technological jobs (*Plate 128*).

In some factories there was initial resistance on the part of men to the employment of women, but in general such prejudice passed fairly rapidly. Many factories, by the middle of the war, presented an appearance of men and women working together equally on jobs demanding equal levels of skill (*Plate 129*).

In life-styles and patterns of behaviour, there were some obvious changes. There is plenty of contemporary comment on the way in which pubs were now filled with women, while in pre-war days there would not have been a woman to be seen. Sometimes both parents were away from home; sometimes young girls were themselves working far from home. Many towns could offer an exotic range of foreign soldiery. Altogether, the war brought a curious but potent mixture of excitement, fear, boredom and opportunity. The First World War had brought about a big upheaval in traditional moral conventions. The Second World War marked a further stage towards the permissive society of today.

3 Women at War: The Old Image

There is controversy as to the true significance of these developments. Some supporters of Women's Lib have argued that whatever changes may have taken place during the war, there was at the end a very sharp reaction in which the traditional feminine image was reimposed upon women. Others have suggested that the war experience was something

130 Jean Rock (aged 19), one of the Windmill Girls, in her Dance of the Seven Veils at the Windmill Theatre's 'Revuedeville'.

of a confidence trick anyway: women were exploited in men's jobs and paid considerably less than men; or, more often, thrust into menial jobs, perhaps kept in the old roles, even if in slightly different environments (army kitchens instead of home kitchens, for example).

It can be said at the outset that there was certainly no sudden reversal in the roles women played. In many cases there were deliberate appeals to the qualities women were felt and, in many cases, felt themselves to possess. For instance, one of the posters appealing for recruits to the Women's Land Army made a special appeal to those 'who liked doing housework'. At best, the WVS, the Emergency Hospital Services, the Auxiliary Ambulances Services, exploited the special talents of women to the fullest. Canteens, British Restaurants and even a National Emergency Washing Service (*Plate 134*) also used women's traditional skills.

Continued emphasis was placed on women as sex symbols and as morale boosters for the troops. One of the legends of the Second World War is provided by the Windmill Theatre in London, with its proud boast 'we never closed'. The Windmill's stock-in-trade, of course, was the nude show, and this, from September 1939 right through the war, it continued to provide for the stay-at-home rich, for the occasional soldier on leave, and for the influx of foreign troops (*Plate 130*). When Michael Balcon made a propaganda film in support of war savings, it seemed perfectly appropriate that the main selling point should be that represented by the title, *The Umpity Poo Girls* (*Plate 131*). Aspiring to the height of fashion was very difficult amid the austerities of war, yet fashion continued to be given great attention in the press, in films and in photographs (*Plate 132*).

131 Some of the cast in the War Savings film, *The Umpity Poo Girls*.

The stupendous appeal of Vera Lynn no doubt lay in the traditional romantic image which she projected in her songs (*Plate 133*). Thus though there is no doubt truth in the notion of women being exploited during the war (as of course were many men – and as, indeed, most people seem to be at some time in all societies), it is quite wrong to think of a complete change of attitude in one direction during the war, followed by a complete reversal after the war. The basic economic and social facts of the war did push women on a definite course, despite the persistence of traditional attitudes. In the Second World War there was nothing quite like the 'votes for women' cry of pre-1914 days, but two other issues came to prominence, 'equal pay' (*Plate 117*) and the employment of married women. On equal pay there was still a very long way to go, though a majority in the House of Commons supported an equal pay amendment to the 1944 Education Bill.

Before the war it was common practice in many professions to sack women as soon as they married. During the war a scarcity of labour inevitably meant that married women were given employment, and the old myths about their unreliability as employees were clearly exposed for what they were. More than this, in a few cases, employers, encouraged by the Government, experimented with the setting up of nurseries which permitted the employment of women with young children. This pointed to an irreversible trend: a government survey conducted among private business at the end of the war, showed a

132   Fashion show at Norman
Hartnell, 1943.

133   Vera Lynn at home, 3
September 1940.

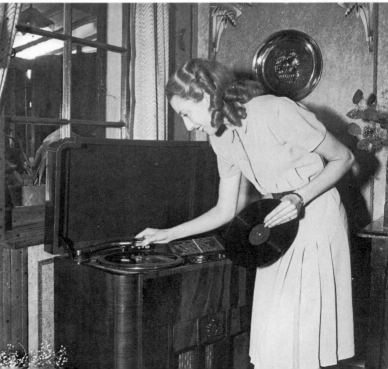

134 The National Emergency Washing Service, sponsored by Lever Brothers. The service was provided for bombed-out women living in rest centres. 1944.

remarkable swing round in opinion with regard to the question of the employment of married women.

Of course many married women, dependent on the miserable allowance paid to soldiers, were badly off: but in general the war meant a new economic and social freedom for women, the experience of which could never be entirely lost. At the same time, a majority of the women who were interviewed made it clear that they still built their hopes on fulfilling the traditional role of being a housewife and raising a family.

4 Science and the Arts

War, the most destructive of all human activities, does not create anything new. It does, however, provide a tremendous incentive to exploit and develop existing knowledge. It also tends to give wider currency to ideas previously held only by a tiny minority.

Principal among the technologies which were greatly developed by the war were: atomic energy, radar, rocket propulsion, jet propulsion, computerization and automation, operational research, plastics and medicine. Penicillin had actually been discovered by Alexander Fleming in 1928, but it took the demand of war to encourage its production on a massive scale (*Plates 135 and 136*). So intensive was the search for containers in which to grow the penicillin mould that yet another wartime problem was created – a shortage of milk bottles!

Britain did not have the resources to develop the full potential of penicillin; the same point applied to proximity fuses, the cavity

135 Mass production of penicillin, October 1943.

136 Sir Alexander Fleming in his laboratory at St Mary's Hospital, Paddington, 17 December 1943.

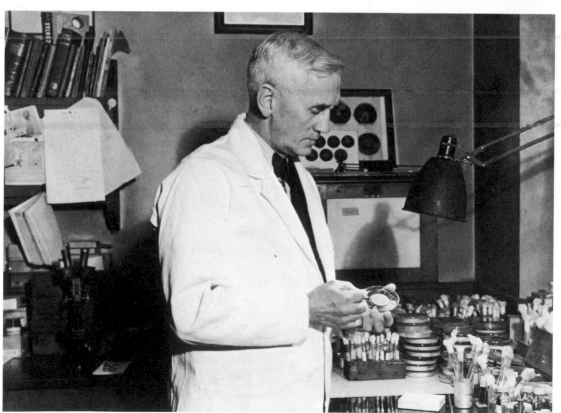

137 Vitamin C expert, Vernon Charley, of Bristol University Research Station, seen here crushing rose hips with a garden roller. His secretary sits on the roller. *Illustrated,* 19 August 1942.

magnetron and, to move from the healing powers of science to science at its most devastating, atomic power. Britain's pioneering work passed to the United States, which largely reaped the benefits. None the less, by the end of the war British society had been given a more definite scientific and technological orientation.

Some publicity was given to the 'boffins', the scientific backroom boys. There was a new accession of prestige to science, and science became popularized and vulgarized. It was known that the Government, very properly, was endeavouring to maintain a high level of nutrition, despite the shortages of basic foodstuffs. From July 1940 the National Milk Scheme provided expectant and nursing mothers and children under five with one pint of milk a day for 2d (less than 1p), or free in cases of need. In late 1942 codliver oil and orange juice were introduced as 'vitamin supplements'. Thus vitamins gained a certain popular attention, along with penicillin and modern weaponry. *Plate 137* is not untypical in its linking of science with the magical antics of a slightly eccentric conjurer. The developing use of mass radiography, which was only just getting under way in the thirties, intensified the war against TB. Particularly effective were the immunization campaigns against typhoid and diphtheria. With regard to the latter serious disease. the number of cases in 1945 was half that of pre-war years.

That war should provide a stimulus to science and technology seems understandable; that it should also provide a stimulus to the arts seems altogether less likely. Yet, because this war was felt to be a war against Nazi barbarity, there was a strong movement towards trying to reinforce the values for which it was felt Western civilization stood.

As early as December 1939, thanks to the private initiative of the Pilgrim Trust, a conference was held at the Board of Education between Lord de la Warr (President of the Board), Lord Macmillan (of the Pilgrim Trust) and Sir Walford Davies and Sir Kenneth Clark (representing music and art respectively), 'to discuss the problems of preserving and promoting cultural activities in wartime'. Out of this conference emerged the Council for the Encouragement for Music and the Arts – always known, in the military style of the day, as CEMA – supported by a grant of £25,000 from the Pilgrim Trust. In April 1940 CEMA was given official government recognition and a subsidy of £50,000. The *Daily Express* went immediately into the attack:

The Government gives £50,000 to help wartime culture. What sort of madness is this? There is no such thing as culture in wartime. Wartime is itself the enemy of culture. And cultural activities, which bring so much benefit to the people in peace, must now be set aside.[47]

The *Daily Express* was quite wrong. As CEMA itself reported, perfectly accurately:

From the beginning, there was no doubt about the demand and, within three months, the Pilgrim Trustees' first, already substantial, grant was doubled by the Treasury. Air-raid conditions intensified the need and gave the work a certain glamour in the eyes of the public. Through the emergency work of artists and organisers during the winter of 1940–41, CEMA began to be known as a name and as an idea.

By the beginning of the third financial year, it seemed to the Pilgrim Trustees that the foundations were fairly laid and that they might, in accordance with their usual policy, withdraw. . . .

The council's third year coincided with a general cessation of air-raids in most parts of the country. The provision of music and drama for war workers and for isolated villages remained a problem; but in the cities there was a return to more normal conditions.

1942 was therefore a time for consolidation as well as for expansion, and the starting point for a considered policy. The council retained its emergency function and its year to year financial basis, but it became possible for the first time to think in terms of the future and to plan with permanent results in mind.

The council has been concerned with the support of old audiences and with the discovery of new ones. The first have been assured a fairly steady, increasing supply of plays, ballets and opera, symphony concerts and chamber music. The guaranteeing of existing companies to continue their normal work and of music subscription clubs to undertake their usual seasons has gone on quietly and with growing success.

138   First air-raid shelter
cinema show, Birmingham
1940.

139   Lunch-hour concert at the
National Gallery, London;
Dame Myra Hess at the piano,
1940.

Opposite:
140   The D'Oyly Carte Opera
Company giving a lunchtime
concert to dock workers at a
communal feeding centre,
Deptford, 25 June 1941.

141   Sadler's Wells Ballet at
Victoria Park, Bethnal Green.
The performance was given
every evening for a week, in
connection with the LCC's
programme for holidays-at-
home entertainments. Precise
date not known.

142 Concert in a northern munitions works: 'a programme was given by employees to their fellow workers, and was broadcast in the Home Service programme. Miss Elsie Simpson, who was down to give one song and tap dance, was asked ten minutes before the broadcast to give three songs and lead community singing to open the broadcast.' Precise date not known.

The second have included groups of village people cut off from each other by wartime conditions, audiences of factory workers in their canteens, and casual audiences gathered together in air-raid shelters and in rest centres for the homeless after air raids. With few exceptions, all of these have made enthusiastic and intelligent audiences, to an extent which confounds some critics. Even the chance audiences assembled during air raids have often, later, developed their own music clubs and dramatic societies, and have presented a permanent demand, in more normal conditions, to be supplied with new material.

Meanwhile, amateur orchestras, choirs, dramatic societies and discussion groups in factories are a constant source of help and inspiration to visiting professionals.[48]

Many factors, of course, contributed to the apparent boom in the arts. For one thing, many people had nothing much else to do. 'Stay at Home' holidays were made the occasion for civic enterprise to provide various cultural and leisure activities. No doubt much of the entertainment was of a rather debased quality, as is strongly suggested by *Plate 142*. None the less government patronage for the arts was something new in Britain, and the work of CEMA continued after the war under the new title of the Arts Council. Out of the war experience were born both the celebrated Bristol Old Vic Company, and what is now the Belgrade Theatre in Coventry.

This is not the place to attempt an assessment of the war's impact on artists, writers and musicians themselves and on their creative output;

our concern is with the war's impact on the relation of the arts and entertainment to the wider society. Suffice it to say that it is no longer possible to accept the older generalizations about the Second World War having failed to produce any equivalent of the War Poets of the First World War. Sensitive and subtle poetry of the Second World War can be seen in such collections as *Poetry of War 1939–1945* (edited by Ian Hamilton, 1965). It is equally true that novelists now gave prominence to the Home Front in a way in which their counterparts of 1914–18, rightly preoccupied with the horrors of trench warfare, had not done.

5 Reversal and Return: D-Day and Flying Bombs, June 1944–March 1945

The D-Day landings, the long awaited opening of the second front in Europe, took place on 6 June 1944, having been delayed by a day because of bad weather. Troops rumbled through the streets on their way to France. It was a pleasant reversal of Dunkirk (*Plate 143*), though there was also a curious inversion of the invasion precautions of 1940 and 1941: a strict, but apparently good-humoured, security had to be maintained in the south-east (*Plate 144*).

In the First World War there had been a division, almost as impenetrable as the trenches and barbed wire of that war, between soldiers and civilians: soldiers in their letters, and on leave, said as little as possible about the quite unbelievably horrific world of trench warfare in Flanders and France. Already in the second war British troops had been involved in the violent campaigns of North Africa, Italy and other Mediterranean theatres; some had suffered the unspeakable terms of war as fought by the Japanese in the Far East. But up to this point war for many men in uniform had meant no more than life in barracks or training camp, tiresome and depressing for some, a pleasant change for others. An ex-librarian, a gunner stationed at Redford barracks in Edinburgh, wrote to one of his lady colleagues at the Bethnal Green Public Library, 'Army life seems to be fag, fags, fun and food, in that order, I have never worked, smoked, laughed, and eaten so much in my life.'[49] The *New Statesman* in January 1943 carried a classified advertisement saying: 'Young Serviceman fond of Beethoven and Beatrice Lillie, stationed outside Birmingham, would relish bath occasional evenings.' Now, at this late stage in the war, the men were marching out to hazardous and bloody battle on the heartland of Europe. For the whole of society, this moment, and the weeks and months which followed, were as poignant as any in any war.

In government circles, retaliation from Hitler in the form of some form of secret weapon (about which the Intelligence Services had had information since 1943) was expected, but the public, in an appallingly wet and nasty summer, was preoccupied with devouring all the

Overleaf:
143 The East End of London made a great effort to supply comforts, such as drinks, cigarettes, soaps, sandwiches and beer, to convoys as they passed through the streets on their way to France. *Illustrated,* 14 June 1944.

144 Security police helping check identities of all civilians in south-east England. Maidstone, 22 May 1944.

available news on the progress of the advance through France. The Baedeker Raids were long since over, and there had been no important daylight raids for many months. Then, at about eleven o'clock on the night of 15 June 1944, the air-raid warning siren, which three years previously had seemed such a permanent part of life, sounded again over London and the south-east. The 'All Clear' did not go till after ten o'clock the following morning. To begin with, the BBC simply referred to 'activity over southern England'. The Government admitted that an attack by 'pilotless planes' had begun; subsequently the description 'flying bombs' was adopted.

The new weapon, the V1, was suitably fiendish. A small plane without a pilot, but carrying a heavy charge of high explosive, it landed whenever its fuel ran out, or sometimes simply dived straight into the ground. Even if shot down, it would still explode. The blast was enormous, and since many came over during the day, when it was impossible for most people to take shelter, the casualties were high.

There were various descriptions of the sinister grating sound made by the V1s, which rose in a most menacing fashion: because of their characteristic, but indefinable, sound, the new weapons were popularly christened 'doodle-bugs' or 'buzz bombs'. As the visual evidence shows only too clearly, the conditions of the Blitz had returned once again. People took to the tube shelters (*Plate 148*), and children, once again, were evacuated (*Plate 147*).

Opposite:
145 V1 attack: a woman rescue worker lifts a child from the ruins of a wrecked building in Buckingham Gate, Victoria, 23 June 1944.

In many ways, the photographic record of this final Blitz is even more dramatic than that of the early one. Photographers no doubt were more practised, and they were now prepared to be rather more daring. The censorship, of course, continued to keep a close watch in making sure that nothing too devastating for morale would be published.

Moving the anti-aircraft defences out towards the coast helped to contain the V1 threat, and in August their launching pads in northern France were overrun by the invading allied forces. Already nearly 6,000 civilians had been killed, and 16,000 more severely injured. The Germans could still fire V1s from piloted planes, and the attacks continued, more sporadically, but spread over a wider geographical area. For example, twenty-seven people were killed in Oldham on Christmas Eve, 1944.

Meantime, a second weapon, the V2, had been brought into service. The first shattering V2 explosion was heard all over London on 8 September. Not till 10 November was it officially admitted that the country was being attacked by rockets. Nearly 3,000 people were killed and over twice that number badly injured in the V2 attacks.

By March 1945 the successful advances on the continent of Europe brought the V1 and V2 menace finally to an end. Devastating bomb-

146 The victim of a flying bomb in the Aldwych lies in the street, covered by the plate of a car wheel, 12 July 1944.

147 Evacuation, 1944: mothers have a last word with their children before the evacuation train leaves Euston, 7 July 1944.

148 People going into the tube shelter in the Elephant and Castle, London 1944.

attacks right at the end of the war, when victory seemed so near, were bound to have an impact on an increasingly war-weary people. Mass Observation characterized the mood as 'general optimism with unstable fear', and quoted an overheard remark:

I'd say my morale was pretty good on the whole, but now and then it seems to come over you, and you realise how awful it all is. A friend of mine at the office was bombed out last night, and she is just sick with horror; she says it's worse than anyone could imagine, women running out of the houses screaming, and others lying in the streets clutching tiny babies. I feel really bad today, after hearing all that.[50]

6 Social Change – or Social Deterioration?

The war ended amid a flurry of White Papers covering all aspects of social reconstruction – 'The White Paper Chase' as it was called. Whatever type of government was in power after the war would be committed to some kind of National Health Service, a Comprehensive Social Insurance Scheme, and an economic policy designed to avoid mass unemployment. In 1944 the famous Butler Education Act was passed, which (whatever its weaknesses) did ensure for the first time that all children would receive some form of secondary education.

Yet for all the genuine good intentions enshrined in the various government papers, the very fact of war necessarily involved a steady deterioration in the quality of life for a vast number of people. Two out of every seven houses were affected more or less seriously by bomb damage. One-fifth of all the country's schools were destroyed, so that although the Education Act marked a great advance in the realm of ideas, in terms of bricks and mortar the war marked quite a serious setback. Altogether 200,000 houses were totally destroyed and a further 250,000 rendered unusable, while maintenance and repairs were neglected in countless others. The total manpower of the building industry steadily declined as men were called away to other tasks: from one million in 1939 it fell to 337,000 in 1945. Over that period only 200,000 houses were built. Houses which were bad slums in 1939, if they had not been severely damaged or totally destroyed, thus forcing their inhabitants to share overcrowded premises with someone else, had become very bad slums indeed by 1945. In an effort to do something about this, the Government introduced prefabricated houses – prefabs (*Plate 152*) – some of which are still lived in today.

On 17 September 1944, the black-out was replaced by a 'dim out', though many people claimed to find it as irritating as the full black-out. Everywhere streets were drab and dingy (*Plate 151*), with the awful gaps of bombed-out buildings (*Plates 100, 101 and 150*). For people on the south coast the uncertain feeling of war remained almost till the very end – photographer Saidman caught this marvellously with his brilliantly set-up picture (*Plate 153*).

149 Middlesex Street, London, after a V2 had dropped, 10 November 1944.

150   Wooden church inside a
bombed shell, Eltham. No
precise date known.

151   The tenor of life in May
1944: boarded-up shops and
peaceful shoppers in Deal.

152   Prefabs in London, 1944.

In speaking of social change it is difficult to get the balance right between the things that changed for the better, the things that changed for the worse, and the things that did not change at all. Undoubtedly there was a strong movement for reform, to which people from all walks of life contributed. Partly because the economy was booming anyway, and partly also because some experiments were conducted in worker participation in management, relations between the employers and employees improved tremendously compared with the 1930s. The old 'hire 'em fire 'em' attitude of the thirties was disappearing, to be replaced by new entrepreneurial attitudes much more sensitive to public opinion and the widespread faith in social solidarity.

But there also remained areas of total resistance to change. In September 1942 the Ministry of Labour drew up a draft memorandum on industrial morale. The memorandum was prepared from evidence provided by regional controllers, industrial relations officers, labour supply inspectors, Employment Exchange managers, welfare officers and factory inspectors. Yet the section on 'relations with management' was drastically amended in a most significant way by the Labour Coordinating Committee of top civil servants, led in this case by Sir Lindsay Scott of the Ministry of Aircraft Production. The original draft declared:

Many employers still cherished the right to discipline their workers and to manage labour in their own way and resented the alleged curtailment of managerial rights. Managements are slow to realise that times are changing and that their relations with their workpeople must change also.

159

POLICE ORDER

We are compelled to clear and close this Cinema **IMMEDIATELY** upon the sounding of a

SHELLING WARNING

No entertainment may be given from the time of such a warning until the sounding of the "SHELLING ALL CLEAR".

You are therefore urged to save your half-ticket. When such a warning is sounded t may be exchanged for a re-admission ticket (AVAILABLE FOR THE SAME ROGRAMME ONLY).

.B. - ON NO ACCOUNT WILL ANY EUEING BE PERMITTED DURING A SHELLING WARNING

REGEN
PRESENTS

THAT UNCERTAI
FEELING A

TO-DAY

The revised version of the memorandum read as follows:

Many employers still consider it important that they should have the right to discipline and manage their workers in their own way, and dislike the curtailment of managerial rights.[51]

In April 1942 the major in charge of the security control office in Glasgow, who also happened to be the son of the managing director of Scotts Shipbuilding Engineering Co., compiled a report on alleged 'slackness' on the part of the Glasgow dockers; Major Brown's report created a ripple through the War Office, the Foreign Office and right up to the War Cabinet, till it was thoroughly squashed by the Ministry of War Transport and the Lord President, Sir John Anderson.[52] There was more than an echo of this in the proceedings of the 1922 Committee of Conservative back-benchers. For example, on 28 May 1941, 'Major Lloyd referred to the maladministration of the Ministry of Labour with special reference to the increasing lack of discipline amongst the dockers of Clydeside'; and there continued to be grumbles about the 'failure to deal with indiscipline in the docks'; 'absenteeism in aircraft factories', 'high wages paid to labour employed on aerodrome construction'; and, again, 'alleged indiscipline on Clydeside'.[53]

The classic expression of faith in the public schools and concern over the recruitment of officers from classes other than the public school élite, is to be found in a notorious letter written by Lt. Colonel R. C. Bingham to *The Times* in January 1941:

Never was the old school tie and the best that it stands for more justified than it is today. Our new armies are being officered by classes of society who are new to the job. The middle, lower middle, and working classes are now receiving the King's commission. These classes, unlike the old aristocratic and feudal (almost) classes who led the old Army, had never had their people to consider. They have never had anyone to think of but themselves. This aspect of life is completely new to them, and they have very largely fallen down on it in their capacity as Army officers.

It is not that they do not wish to carry out this part of their duties properly, but rather that they do not know how to begin. Man management is not a subject which can be 'taught'; it is an attitude of mind, and with the old school tie men this was instinctive and part of the philosophy of life. These new young officers will be just as brave and technically efficient, but they have been reared in an atmosphere in which the State spoon feeds them from cradle to grave and no-one feels any responsibility for his fellowmen. This, Sir, is a sad reflection on our educational system.[54]

Bingham was suspended from his duties, but his views were not really so different from that of the orthodoxy prevailing throughout the war. A special committee, the Fleming Committee, was set up to consider the position of public schools, but its terms of reference made it clear that there must be no question of abolishing them; in fact the main recommendation of the resulting report was simply that 25 per cent of the places in public schools should be made available to children from poorer backgrounds. The most sophisticated argument

153 *That Uncertain Feeling:* cinema and shelling warning, 18 May 1944.

appeared in the *Economist*, which in July 1944 declared the public schools to be the best schools in the world, acquitted them of deliberately fostering snobbery, and remarked that 'the trouble is not that the Public Schools are schools of leadership, but that their exclusive social standing inevitably forces all other schools to be, in a greater or lesser degree, schools of followership.'[55] R. A. Butler ensured that in the discussions leading up to the Education Act of 1944, Conservative policy groups should not involve themselves in discussing the public schools. In Labour Party discussions, too, public schools were virtually ignored; but then, of course, many prominent Labour personalities were ex-public school-boys.

The deliberate wartime policy of providing mothers and children with welfare foods and food supplements was undoubtedly successful, not only in maintaining levels of nutrition, but in generally providing a better start in life than many children of the depression had had. Still, no power in the world could force mothers to take up their allocation, nor could it stop them, if they so desired, from pouring their codliver oil down the drain. In April 1944 the Wartime Social Survey conducted an enquiry on behalf of the Ministry of Food into the use being made of fruit juices and codliver oil. Out of a small, but systematically chosen sample of under 900 nursing mothers and mothers with children under five, 73 per cent were taking orange juice either for themselves or for their children. As for codliver oil (containing vitamins A and B) 62 per cent were giving this to their children or taking it for themselves. Four-fifths of the children taking Ministry of Food fruit juice and codliver oil took it regularly every day.

According to the survey, only one-third of the children who took it actively disliked codliver oil; as children grew older they tended to refuse to take it. 'More than a third of the mothers admitted that they do not reserve the fruit juice for the child which is entitled to it, but share it among other members of their family. This number might be even greater in reality. A quarter of the mothers who take codliver oil share it also.'[56] The survey also revealed that only half of the mothers interviewed had the right ideas about the health value of the fruit juice. There was something touchingly British in their belief that its main function was as a laxative. The health value of codliver oil was better appreciated, no doubt because of the nastiness of its taste.

CHAPTER SIX

1945 and After

I VE-Day

Amid the ruins of Berlin, Adolf Hitler committed suicide on 30 April 1945. On 4 May the German forces in north-western Europe surrendered to General Montgomery at Lüneburg Heath. On 7 May the German Supreme Command surrendered at Rheims. 8 May was designated as VE-Day – Victory in Europe Day (the war against the Japanese still continued).

There had been no jubilation at the outbreak of war, only a sense of moral release. It is impossible to generalize about reactions to VE-Day. Of course, there was rejoicing. For the first time for many long weary years there was floodlighting of public buildings and statues; restaurants and cinemas and theatres were fully lit up. Indeed, it was said that some children were terrified by the unexpected amount of light. The most powerful source for the nature of the VE-Day celebrations is to be found in the Ministry of Information: *War Pictorial News*, Issue 213, item 2B of May 1945. The scenes are of great patriotic jubilation, together with impressive shots of Churchill, the Royal Family, and other political leaders appearing on the balcony at Buckingham Palace. Yet the enormous emotional impact of this piece of source material derives very largely from the very effective use of the sound track of Elgar's Pomp and Circumstance march No. 1: in this particular case still (and silent!) photographs are perhaps more revealing.

Plate 154 shows the rather stylized aspect of the celebrations; *Plate 155* shows people as pensive rather than jubilant; but *Plate 156* shows the characteristic scenes of soldiers and girls, which were featured so much in the press and which are the archetype of what victory celebrations should look like.

Victory, of course, was expected, and there was some frustration over the time it took to issue the final announcement, which did not come till twenty minutes to eight on the night of 7 May. But whatever deeper feelings people may have had, there could be no doubt that 8 May was a day in which almost everyone gave full rein to the immediate feelings of relief and national triumph. It was a mixture of festival, fair, Wakes Week and rag. For many children it was the first ever opportunity to savour the delights of bonfires and fireworks. For many adults much of the movement was basically aimless, but there

Opposite:
154   VE-Day celebrations in London: *Evening News* vans waiting to rush out papers, 8 May 1945.

155   VE-Day scenes in Regent Street, London.

156   VE-Day scenes near Buckingham Palace.

were bands, music, flags and a moderate amount of drinking. The tiny core of a thousand or so who were resorting to the tubes and the deep shelters, probably because they felt they had nowhere else to go, still did so. There were many foreign troops and representatives of newly liberated (and thoroughly devastated) Europe. For the bereaved, as always, much of the rejoicing must have been especially painful.

Yet the celebrations were real. A level-headed civil servant, now returned to suburban Surrey after his wartime evacuation to Lancashire, seems, in a matter-of-fact sort of way, to have got it right: 'We went to London on VE night and joined the singing and shouting crowds in the West End. We put a Union Jack on the top gable of our house and strung coloured lights round the edge of the roof. All the houses were decorated and there was dancing round the island in Claygate lane. Everyone was very happy.'[57] And Churchill got it as right as anyone could in a few sentences, when he told the crowd outside Buckingham Palace: 'This is your victory. It is the victory of the cause of freedom in every land. In all our long history we have never seen a greater day than this. Everyone, man or woman, has done their best.'

2 The General Election

It was widely believed that the war against Japan might well go on for another couple of years. Churchill was keen to keep together his national coalition, but the Labour Party which, rightly, felt that he was lukewarm on social reform, was eager to return to peacetime politics. In the end Churchill issued the Labour leaders with a rather petulant ultimatum: if they would not stay with him in the Government, then they must face an immediate general election. Interestingly, he toyed too with the idea of having a referendum on whether there should be a general election or not.[58]

Public-opinion polls showed that there had been a steady movement towards Labour during the war, and predicted a Labour victory; but nobody paid any attention to polls in those days. It was generally thought that Churchill's great prestige as the victorious war leader would give the Conservatives a satisfactory majority, though, in fact, as we have seen, there was a good deal of hostility to Churchill in certain areas. Churchill's procession through his own and other constituencies was almost entirely a triumphal tour (*Plate 157*). By contrast, Attlee seemed mild and self-effacing, if quietly authoritative (*Plate 158*).

During the election period, the country was administered by a 'caretaker' government of purely Conservative composition: it passed the act introducing Family Allowances. Public-opinion polls showed that the issue which most concerned people was housing. Labour effectively presented itself as the party most strongly committed to social reform.

157 Winston Churchill waves
to the crowd after speaking at
the Broadway, Waltham Cross,
on an electioneering tour, 2 July
1945.

158 Clement Attlee addresses
constituents in his own seat of
Limehouse, during an election
eve canvassing tour, 1945.

Mass communications, particularly radio, played a bigger part in this election than in any previous one. It was not so much that Labour exploited the device more effectively than the Conservatives, but that the political broadcasts brought out more clearly than the printed word could ever have done that Labour had clearly thought-out plans, while the Conservatives could rely only on the appeal of Churchill and national victory. Churchill himself seemed to rely only on rhetoric, and when he said of the party headed by Attlee and Morrison, two of the most inoffensive looking little men ever to have led a political party, that 'they would have to fall back on some sort of Gestapo', he reduced to absurdity the essential difference between Labour and Conservative: the point was driven home by Attlee's calm and constructive speech of the following evening. Newsreel interviews with the political leaders also made their contribution: Churchill appeared gloomy, and could only speak of the terribly difficult times ahead; Attlee seemed alert and optimistic, and sure that the efforts which had been put in to winning the war could be canalized into building a better society.

Polling took place on 5 July 1945. Because of the difficulties of collecting and counting the serving men's votes, it was some weeks before the results were announced. Labour had a landslide majority in Parliament, rather less than 50 per cent of the total votes, but a slight overall majority when averaged out over all the constituencies which they contested. The figures were: Labour 393, Conservatives 213, Liberals 12, ILP 3, Communists 2, Independents 14. Labour had 47·8 per cent of the total votes cast, the Conservatives 39·8 per cent, the Liberals 9 per cent, and the others 3·4 per cent. The discrepancy between Labour's parliamentary majority and its slightly less impressive majority in the country was partly due to the workings of the single member constituency system, and partly due to the fact that the Conservatives put up more candidates than did Labour (618 to 599): Labour's average percentage vote per candidate standing was 50·4, that of the Conservatives 40·1.

Labour won because of the colossal mood for radical change engendered by the war, not just among working-class voters, but, much more critically, among middle-class voters, one-third of whom, it has been estimated, voted Labour, thus providing the real key to Labour's triumph. Labour won because, by conviction and composition, it was the party most likely to respond in full to that mood, and because the limelight of office had banished the lingering shadows of doubt about its fitness to rule.

The results were variously received. One crusty Tory described the Labour members overflowing the benches of the House of Commons as 'just like a crowd of damned constituents'. Eddie Lawrence, the civil servant from the Ministry of Agriculture whose description of VE-night we noted above, continued his letter as follows:

But the happiness and exuberance of spirits was brought to an abrupt end by the results of the General Election. The gloom and despondency that prevailed in Hinchley Wood could not have been greater if we had lost the war. The idea of some of our big industries owned to a large extent by foreigners being owned by the country instead, was nauseating to this patriotic community. . . . Being a Civil Servant, I have no politics, but I must confess I was somewhat amused at this local depression. They derived some solace, however, from the fact that the local Conservative candidate, Commander Marsden, was returned though with by no means an overwhelming majority. . . .

Viewed from the inside, the civil service takes an impressive view of the drive of the new Labour Ministers. Our own man in particular has pleased the farmers with his forthright manner and energy. I don't know he has pleased *us* so much, as new legislation means more work, and we are continually loosing [*sic*] our staff, a large percentage being temporary married women.

The fear of nationalisation seems to be very real. Why, I do not know.[59]

Lawrence's sister-in-law wrote: 'We were certainly staggered by the election result especially as I live and worked in a very Conservative atmosphere – the end of the world would have occasioned only a little. more alarm.'[60]

It is said that when President Truman of the United States met King George VI at Portsmouth in July, he remarked, 'You've had a revolution', to which the King replied, 'Oh no! we don't have those here.' A few days later, the King's reaction is said to have been: 'What I say is "Thank God for the civil servants".'

In the Labour Government, Attlee (Prime Minister), Dalton (Chancellor of the Exchequer) and Cripps (President of the Board of Trade) were all distinctly upper-class figures. One of the most pleasantly ironic comments on the general election result is to be found in Attlee's old school magazine, the *Haileyburian and Imperial Service Chronicle* (9 November 1945).

Unfortunately the results of the General Election last July only became known after our last number had gone to print, and so, except for a last minute insertion, we were unable to make any mention of the political success of six of our Old Boys.

We should, therefore, like to take this opportunity of congratulating E. P. Smith (Conservative), A. L. Ungoed Thomas (Labour), J. W. Snow (Labour), Geoffrey de Freitas (Labour), and C. P. Mayhew (Labour) on their elections to Parliament, and, in addition, J. W. Snow on his appointment as Vice-Chamberlain of His Majesty's Household; Geoffrey de Freitas on his appoint [*sic*] as Parliamentary Private Secretary to the Prime Minister; and C. P. Mayhew on being appointed P.P.S. to Mr. Herbert Morrison.

But the School is still more honoured by Mr. C. R. Attlee's appointment as Prime Minister, Minister of Defence, and First Lord of the Treasury. This is the first time that any Old Boy has ever filled such high office, and on behalf of the old School, many hundreds of O.H's and O.I.S.C's, and all those connected with Haileybury and the Imperial Service College we extend our heartiest congratulations to Mr. Attlee, proud that he is a son of Haileybury, and confident that he will not fail his high trust.[61]

3 VJ-Day

Britain had long since lost any control over the development and use of atomic weapons. On 6 August 1945 the Americans dropped the first atomic bomb on Hiroshima; on 9 August a second bomb was dropped

159 VJ-Day: dancing in the streets; note the posters about VJ-Day and China in the background, left. There is one sailor dancing, but in the main the girls have to dance with each other.

on Nagasaki. A new shadow had fallen across the world; British newspapers were full of screaming headlines, people's conversations heavy with foreboding.

Eddie Lawrence concluded his letter with a reference to his brother-in-law, who, he wrote, 'is particularly depressed. I think he regards the labour government and the atom bomb as two inescapable evils, either being certain to bring about his demise.' On 28 October, his sister-in-law wrote: 'I think the papers are now most depressing everyone quarrelling and the shadow of the atom bomb hanging over everything.'[62]

Whatever the rights and wrongs of the almost casual way in which the first atomic weapons were brought into use, Japanese surrender, which took place on 14 August, was certainly speeded up beyond all earlier expectation.

160 VJ-Day. Montgomery's visit to Lambeth: girl injured by a policeman's horse. *News Chronicle* photograph, 16 August 1945.

Now, although the Japanese had always seemed more remote, the country could celebrate VJ-Day. On the whole, this seems to have been a more carefully prepared occasion, with dancing in the streets (*Plate 159*) and parades (*Plate 161*). In the days that followed, General Montgomery visited various places as a conquering hero. Of course, all such mass occasions have their tragic side. A *News Chronicle* photographer was quick to snap the rather sadly moving picture of a little girl injured by a policeman's horse (*Plate 160*).

A Liverpool businessman concluded his war diary in the following manner, not unreminiscent of the reactions of front-line soldiers to the Armistice in 1918 – but then in this war civilians, too, had been in the front line:

16 Aug. 1945. V.J. Day. Victory over Japan day and a public holiday. Went down to West Kirby in the morning and found council workmen putting up

161   VJ-Day crowds in Piccadilly Circus. The statue of Eros is still missing and the fountain had been boarded up throughout the war; and War Savings posters are much in evidence. On the other hand, it is clear that the bright lights, traditionally associated with Piccadilly Circus, are back. *Daily Mail* photograph.

flags in a half hearted manner. No signs of joy, of enthusiasm, no cheering crowds, all shops shut and the streets almost deserted. I could not help but contrast the feeling and apathy with the day peace was declared at the end of the First World War when the streets of Manchester were packed to suffocation by delirious crowds, all trams cars stopped and the pubs closed. Maybe most of us are mentally and physically exhausted; maybe we have become so accustomed to living under war-time restraints, we have not yet realised that fighting has stopped. I can speak only for myself on this day. I feel no elation no uplifting of spirit, only a sort of dumb inarticulate thankfulness that the hell of war, the killing, the misery is over; that Anne and I are alive and well.

At night we went to Caldy Hill to see the bonfires blazing on the distant Welsh hills. What pleased us more was to see the opposite side of the Dee twinkling with thousands of street lamps and lighted windows. So we went home, opened wide the curtains and switched on every light in the house. More than anything else did this action, one taken by nearly everyone, bring home to us the fact that the war had ended.[63]

Writing of the immediate post-VJ-Day period, Eddie Lawrence's brother-in-law, John King, struck a sour note:

London is one solid mass of people, you can hardly walk along the pavements, one begins to wonder if anyone does any work at all, something seems wrong somewhere when the country is crying out for effort that so many people are able to mill aimlessly about town all day – they can't all be on holiday.[64]

4 The Aftermath

The Labour Government proceeded quickly to pass the series of major Acts of Parliament which meant that by 1948 Britain was a full Welfare State: the National Insurance and the National Health Service Acts of 1946 and the National Assistance Act of 1948. It also nationalized most of the major industries, though it did not thereby add much to the worker's sense of involvement, nor contribute to diminishing the social divide between management and worker. Other noteworthy pieces of social legislation were the Housing Acts of 1946, the Town and Country Planning Act of 1947, the Children Act of 1948, and the Legal Aid and Advice Act of 1949.

For many, there was a sense of purpose about these immediate post-war years, and although the war had left its scars, and its sense of human tragedy (altogether 355,000 British soldiers and civilians had been killed), for the mass of the people life was a good deal better than ever it had been in the 1930s. Austerity and rationing remained. The high wartime level of taxation continued.

Robert Hamer's Ealing Studios film *It Always Rains on Sunday* (1948) perhaps best captured the drabness of life in this period (*Plate 162*). Brooding over this sleazy crime film is the institution of corporal punishment – particularly the 'cat'. It was in fact in 1948 that the Criminal Justice Act carried out what had been intended by the Chamberlain Government in 1939 when war intervened: the abolition of judicial corporal punishment.

162   The centre of Plymouth, 1945.

Apart from universal bomb destruction, other elements spilled over from the war into peacetime. For example, it was some time before German prisoners of war, employed in various menial civilian tasks, disappeared from the scene (*Plate 163*). Opinion surveys suggested that, though not particularly friendly towards the POWs, the British public had no very strong feelings about them; soldiers and ex-soldiers expressed markedly more sympathetic attitudes. However, the first full revelation, during the last months of the war, of the barbarities of the German concentration and extermination camps – in the cinemas people could see some of the shots taken by army cameramen as the advancing Allies overran the camps – brought a new intensification of anti-German feeling. War factories, military bases, RAF stations, barbed wire, pill boxes, Nissen huts, stretches of concrete, all of these remained, eyesores upon the landscape.

Housing was the issue on which most people felt most strongly. Aneurin Bevan, the Minister of Health, promised a high standard of

163 German POWs cleaning up
at Victoria Gardens, London.
No precise date known.

housing for all, so that it should not perpetuate class distinctions (he spoke of re-creating the social structure of pre-industrial villages, which showed that his history was as inadequate as, unfortunately, his housing policies turned out to be). Official publications on housing, as on other social matters, were informed by a new generous tone, which contrasted sharply with the means-test attitudes of the thirties. But it was much more difficult actually to build the houses, and many young couples had nothing to look forward to except a lengthy housing queue. Prefabs were to be seen everywhere (*Plate 164*).

164 Prefabricated town on the Isle of Dogs, 16 January 1946. The jaunty caption to go with this Keystone Press photograph read: 'In the 1940–41 blitz Cubitt Town, on the Isle of Dogs, was almost wiped out. Now on the old site, London's first wholly prefabricated town has sprung up. There are three hundred of these squat, box-shaped buildings, of which two hundred are already occupied. More are going up. The old Cubitt Town residents returning from evacuation say they are delighted with the new town.'

165 Housewives' protest meeting against bread scheme, Central Hall, Westminster, 8 July 1946. The meeting was called by the British Housewives League, formed by Mrs Irene Lovelock.

The new Government had many real achievements to its credit. In some areas it was unlucky; it was also incompetent. Bread had been a staple foodstuff all through the war (*Plates 70 and 71*); in 1946, for the first time in British history, John Strachey, the Minister of Food, had to introduce bread rationing (*Plate 165*). The winter of 1946–47 was an abysmally harsh one. Coal and other fuels became as scarce as ever they had been during the war. The Minister of Fuel was Emanuel Shinwell, and the Conservatives coined the slogan: 'Shiver with Shinwell, and starve with Strachey'.

Although by-elections, and indeed the general election of 1950 (when, although the Conservatives gained many seats, Labour's total vote rose), showed that the Government continued to have much

166 Elephant and Castle, 8 January 1949. 'A view of the meeting-place of six traffic arteries of London . . . where the emblem of the Cockney world looks down on London's liveliest domain.'

popular support, a number of strongly anti-Labour pressure groups were founded. One such was the British Housewives League (*Plate 165*).

Finally, it is well worth looking closely at London's famous Elephant and Castle as it was in January 1949 (*Plate 166*). There is plenty of bomb damage, certainly, but the basic structure of this historic spot is intact. Today the Elephant and Castle is a horrible mess of hideous high-rise buildings. War was destructive, but perhaps not nearly so destructive as the 'redevelopment policies' of the 1950s and 1960s – though it was during the war itself that the new breed of property developers first saw the chance to convert damaged residential areas into commercial properties.

CHAPTER SEVEN.

The Social Consequences of the Second World War

Was the Second World War, in a genuine non-ironic sense, a 'People's War'? Was it for the ordinary people who lived through it a time of simple heroism, a high point in their lives, a period now to be spoken of with reverence? Was the war followed by a 'People's Peace', as Common Wealth urged that it should be, or did 1945 mark, as the present editor of the *New Statesman* has argued, 'the greatest restoration of traditional values since 1660 [the date of the restoration of Charles II after the Cromwellian interlude]'?[65] In sum, did the war bring about social change? If so, what kind of change? – were things better for the trade unions, but worse for the country, or for the middle class? – was Lord Croft, Under-Secretary at the War Office, in the end right when he denounced the Beveridge report as likely to reduce 'industry to a Tom Tiddler's ground'? If there was change, *how* did it come about? What, in the wider perspective, was the social significance of the war?

Any snappy generalization such as 'People's War' is open to all sorts of qualifications. Yet four pungent reasons can be given for arguing that the Second World War genuinely was a 'People's War'. First, for a relatively short period during the Blitz ordinary people were in the front line, bearing the direct brunt of enemy fire power; second, over the longer period of the whole war, direct participation in all aspects of the national effort by ordinary people was absolutely vital, first to survival, then to victory; third, the war for the first time gave a genuine influence to individuals who believed themselves to be spokesmen, not of the establishment, but of the people – film-makers like John Baxter and Thorold Dickinson, publicists like J. B. Priestley and Ritchie Calder, temporary civil servants like D. N. Chester; and fourth, for all the powerful resistances that remained, there was in all sections of society a movement in favour of radical social reform.

It is not possible to give so clear or positive an answer to the question about simple heroism, about the war as a high point in the ordinary person's life. The truth has certainly been coloured by propaganda and by hindsight. More than that, the truth on such a subject must necessarily be complex. It is important to remember that human beings can entertain quite conflicting emotions at the same time: a very real and a very understandable fear could co-exist with a strong conviction that Hitler was an enemy who must be defeated whatever the cost.

Disgruntlement and even bitterness in the contemporary writings of civilians is no more surprising than that shown in many servicemen's letters during the First World War; and just as these servicemen continued, however unhappily, to carry out their patriotic duties in the trenches, so too it was possible for East End victims to feel at the end of the day that their cause was Britain's, however badly Britain had treated them. There is real evidence of the heroism, the high active morale, and the much vaunted humour. Whose idea it was to put up patriotic flags on damaged buildings is not known; but they certainly appeared. No doubt slogans of the type, 'No damage only a few panes', were copied, and recopied; but they certainly also appeared. It does no good to glorify the Second World War, or to minimize the grinding boredom, the real grievances and the terrible suffering. But it does no good either to deny the exaltation, the sense of achievement and the heightening of consciousness.

There were many upper-class figures in the Labour Government of 1945. In the main, it preserved the forms of collaboration with industry developed during the war and it worked amicably with the traditional Civil Service. Nothing was done about the public schools. Nationalization of major industries did little to change the balance of power between management and workers. Yet if we compare the attitudes towards social questions and towards class rampant in the 1930s with those of the late 1940s, we can immediately see that much had changed. The keynote of the new welfare state legislation was 'universalism' – that is to say the new services were to include all members of the community so that there should not be first-class service for those who paid and second-class service for those who did not. In a way the working class after 1945 assumed a position in the social structure rather similar to that assumed by the middle class after 1832. Then the middle class and now the working class seemed happy on the whole to continue to be governed in political and in economic matters by their social superiors; at the same time, the working class after 1945 was clearly recognized as an important segment in the community, whose aspirations could not be ignored.

Those writers who exaggerate the revolutionary nature of the changes during the war are all the more disappointed at the apparent absence of change after the war. In fact, as we have seen, there were all through the war resistances to change. Naturally, the resistances continued into the post-war period, and ultimately gained in strength as memories of the war faded. No change comes about without effort on the part of individuals: but the war at least, in a manner in which no individual could foresee, tipped the balance of circumstances so as to make them more susceptible to further change. Because his is a purely political study, Paul Addison lays too much stress on May 1940 as a turning point.[66] Real social change only developed over a longer period and was then, perhaps, somewhat more significant than he seems to allow.

Societies do not normally proceed along a straight line towards some ideal condition. Furthermore, changes which may appear to be in the interest of individuals or groups – often quite substantial groups – within society may in the long run not be conducive to the health or survival of society. There is force in the argument that the particular mix of what changed and what did not change bequeathed by the Second World War was to have serious long-term consequences for Britain's economic development. One effect of the war was quite definitely to enhance the bargaining power of labour; yet the entire trade-union structure, together with the earlier twentieth-century assumptions which went with it, remained substantially unchanged. Industrial relations were now conducted in a much friendlier spirit, but the structure of management too was little changed. There was a feeling that institutions having survived the test of war and thus, it was argued, having proved themselves, did not need to be changed; there was perhaps also a feeling that 'having won the war' the British people deserved to be allowed to relax and enjoy the fruits of victory.

A more persuasive thesis may be that the war enforced some stark geo-political realities. A small country with dwindling natural resources could no longer go on behaving like a giant world power. The Empire had no clothes. But unfortunately the nation's leaders failed to perceive this truth in time and make the adjustments that were necessary.

These are in part matters of conjecture, and certainly not matters about which to moralize. For the central point is that the changes which did take place were brought about through mechanisms touched off by the war, rather than by the conscious action of any politicians or social leaders. It is in this connection that I come back to the four dimensions of war I outlined at the beginning of the book. Theories should never be imposed on history; but they should be welcomed if they do genuinely help us to make sense of the flux and muddle of historical development. Professor K. L. Nelson, in looking at various wars and American society, has suggested that the analysis of the impact of war might be integrated into the theory of modernization: that everywhere in industrialized countries there has been a steady movement towards mass society, centralized government and sophisticated technology. War is then seen as a central force in accelerating modernization.[67] The thesis may be true with regard to the United States and the Second World War; but for Britain it is far too simplistic, since the results of the war were very complex, in some respects confirming traditional attitudes as well as, in other respects, encouraging new ones. Thus I turn to my four dimensions of war.

The *destructiveness* of the war is readily apparent; so too is its *disruptiveness*, if one thinks of the way in which people were projected into all sorts of new life situations and patterns of behaviour, rather different from those they would have continued to follow in times of peace. But more than that, the very destructiveness produced a strong drive in favour of reconstruction: 'bombs', said the Federation of British Industries, 'have made builders of us all.'

The test of war can be seen in the creation of the Emergency Hospital Scheme, designed to overcome the deficiencies in the old hospital system which the war starkly revealed. It can be seen in the collapse of the old style of conservatism, exhibited in the leadership of Neville Chamberlain, and the emergence of the new conservatism of the Tory Reform Committee. The *participation* effect can be seen in the gains made by women and by the working class.

The *psychological* dimension is more complex and links up closely with the other three, particularly in fostering a mood favourable to change. One aspect which is specially worth attention is the manner in which war seems to encourage the sense of belonging to an 'in-group' and to strengthen hostility towards 'out-groups'. Taking a total view of the nation, it seems to be true that there was an enhancement of the sense of being British and, of course, a canalizing of hostility towards the enemy, Nazi Germany. This sentiment was strongest among the articulate middle and upper classes, and often took the form of a desire to improve the lot of those lower down the social scale. There could also be, as we have seen, an enhancement, for example, of the sense of Scottishness; and there was certainly an enhancement of the sense of belonging to the working class or to a particular trade union. Indeed, in the modern phrase which I have used once or twice, there was, among different groups, a 'heightening of consciousness'. This meant that just when society as a whole, or its ruling groups, were prepared and willing to make concessions to those lower down the scale, those same under-privileged groups were more willing than ever to stand up and make demands on their own behalf. These two processes came together to join in the movement towards radical reform.

Yet the psychological, 'in-group, 'one-nation' feeling could also cut across the movement for reform. Many former radicals allowed the harmonious spirit of wartime to blunt the edge of their reforming zeal. In 1943 eleven Labour MPs visited five top public schools, Christ's Hospital, Eton, Harrow, Charterhouse and Winchester. 'What did we find?' asked George Muff, MP for East Hull. 'We found an utter absence of snobbery. After all, the average normal boy is the same all England over. Whether rich or poor, the young lad has to be made, under duress, to wash his neck as well as his face. . . . there was a fine simplicity of living. . . . These public schools breed character.' Mr Muff was at one with Lord Fleming, the *Economist* and indeed with Colonel Bingham. His unrevolutionary plea was to ask that 'the door . . . be . . . at least ajar for the boy who has passed the entrance examination to the local grammar school, whose parents are ready for their boy to go to a boarding school, and who is temperamentally suitable.'[68] This received attitude was ratified in a film of 1948, *The Guinea Pig*, which after beginning on a note of class antagonism, turned into a hymn of praise for public-school traditions and education.

Bernard Miles's *Chance of a Lifetime* (1950), in which workers take over a factory, then give up because the running of it is all too much for them, is also revealing of a whole set of received attitudes. Just before the 1945 election Bevin had expressed to Attlee the hope that the war had removed 'the inferiority complex amongst our people'.[69] But a sardonic Australian observer had noted in February 1942 that 'the English will put up with anything if someone wearing an Eton or Harrow tie tells them it's good for them!'[70] Slowly, over five years of war, opinions did change: but there were many entrenched attitudes which could easily reassert themselves in the years of peace.

Since the discontinuity provided by the Second World War there has been a further upheaval: the period of the late fifties and the early sixties – living standards took a further leap upwards; there was release from the gloom of the immediate post-war era; and a great flood of new consumer goods and one or two significant technological innovations, such as the development of the contraceptive pill. This period saw a revolution in manners and morals greater than that brought about by the war. More recently still, the country has moved into a period of economic crisis which makes even the social legacies of Beveridge and the war era seem tatty and inadequate.

It is not surprising, therefore, that even if the war can be held up as a model period of national unity and purpose, and indeed as a period of social reform, historians find it increasingly difficult to argue that it ushered in a long-term era of continuing change. The reality, this book has suggested, lies somewhere among these assertions. The majority of the British people were better off after the Second World War than they had been before it. We can continue to learn much from a study of the war and its aftermath. But the era of which they formed a part is now definitely over.

Text Notes

1 Margesson Papers, MRGN 1/5. Churchill College, Cambridge.
2 *British Medical Journal*, June 1940.
3 Mass Observation file 3073.
4 Brinton-Lee Diary, 15 August–1 September 1937. Imperial War Museum.
5 Haslam Collection, 1 September 1939. Imperial War Museum.
6 H. A. Penny Diary, 1 September 1939 Imperial War Museum.
7 Mel Calman in B. S. Johnson (ed.), *The Evacuees* (1963); pp 35–36.
8 Mass Observation file 11.
9 Mass Observation file 11.
10 Yates correspondence, 6 October 1939. Imperial War Museum.
11 War Diaries of Nurse Phipps (typescript), June 1940. Imperial War Museum.
12 Mass Observation file 139.
13 Mass Observation file 174.
14 Monckton Papers, Bodleian Library, Dept M.T.3. Docs. 38–40.
15 'Seven weeks of Internment in England'. Undated, unsigned memorandum (typescript). Liddell Hart Archives.
16 Liddell Hart Archives, 1/112/29, etc.
17 Brinton-Lee Diary, 15–21 September 1940.
18 Mass Observation file 392.
19 Mass Observation file 431.
20 H. E. Strong Papers, Box 4.
Imperial War Museum.
21 Brinton-Lee Diary, 8–15 September 1940.
22 Haslam Collection, 5 January 1941.
23 McHutchison Diary, 23 March 1941. Imperial War Museum.
24 Hilda Neal Diary, 18 September 1940. Imperial War Museum.
25 Archway Letter, 13 September 1940. Imperial War Museum.
26 H. A. Penny Diary, 12 September, 11 October 1940.
27 PRO CAB 67/9/(41) 44.
28 PRO CAB 66/12 WP (40) 107.
29 PRO CAB 68/7/ WP (R) (40) 196, 10 October 1940.
30 Mass Observation file 431
31 Hilda Neal Diary, 11 September 1940.
32 H. E. Strong Papers, 17 September 1940.
33 Yates correspondence, 27 September 1940.
34 Laski-Huebsch correspondence, 4 November 1940. British Library of Political and Economic Science and Library of Congress.
35 Mass Observation file 3073.
36 Vera Reid's Cameos of 1939–41, 13 May 1941. Typescript on microfilm. Imperial War Museum.
37 T. E. B. Clarke, *Where I came In* (1974), p. 133.
38 Mass Observation file 508.
39 Marie Paneth, *Brand Street* (1944), pp. 71–72.

40 Copy of a letter to the Minister of Transport from a woman in Southampton, September 1940. PRO (Ashridge), HLG 900/59.

41 Quoted by Angus Calder, *The People's War* (1969), p. 317.

42 *Current Affairs*, 5 December 1942.

43 Beveridge to Mrs R. H. Tawney, 29 July 1941; Beveridge Papers, BEV IIa 78. British Library of Political and Economic Science.

44 *House of Commons Debates*, 9 October 1941.

45 Beveridge to G. Mowat, 12 June 1942 (copy); Beveridge Papers, BEV VIII 31. British Library of Political and Economic Science.

46 PRO S.I.C. (32), 20 May 1942.

47 *Daily Express*, 13 April 1940.

48 *CEMA Report*, 1942–43.

49 Gunner Jack Luck to Miss E. Evans, 30 March 1942; Evans Papers. Imperial War Museum.

50 Mass Observation file 2121.

51 Draft Memorandum on Industrial Morale, 16 September 1942. PRO L.C.C. (42) 59. Bevin Papers, BEVN 2/13. Churchill College, Cambridge.

52 The report, entitled 'Morale of Allied Seamen', dated 27 April 1942, was circulated to the War Cabinet as W.P. (42) 234. The complete file is PRO CAB 123/198.

53 Quoted by Philip Goodhart, *The 1922* (1973), pp. 107–108.

54 *The Times*, 15 January 1941.

55 The *Economist*, 29 July 1944.

56 Wartime Social Survey, *Food Supplement: An Enquiry for the Ministry of Food*, April 1944.

57 E. Lawrence to H. E. Strong, 23 December 1945. Strong Papers.

58 ATL 2/2 Attlee Papers. Churchill College, Cambridge.

59 E. Lawrence to H. E. Strong, 23 December 1945. Strong Papers.

60 Doris King to H. E. Strong, 28 October 1945. Strong Papers.

61 *Haileyburian and Imperial Service Chronicle*, 9 November 1945.

62 E. Lawrence to H. E. Strong, 23 December 1945, and Doris King to Strong, 28 October 1945. Strong Papers.

63 N. F. Ellison Diary, 16 August 1945. Imperial War Museum.

64 John King to H. E. Strong, 11 September 1945. Strong Papers.

65 Anthony Howard, 'We are the Masters Now', p. 31 in M. Sissons and P. French (eds), *The Age of Austerity* (1963).

66 Paul Addison, *The Road to 1945* (1975), pp. 17, 14.

67 K. L. Nelson, *The Impact of War on American Life* (1971), Introduction.

68 *The Times*, 8 July 1943.

69 Bevin Papers, BEVN 311. Churchill College, Cambridge.

70 John Hughes to Elizabeth Strong, 11 February 1942. Strong Papers.

Note on Further Reading

Angus Calder, *The People's War* (1969), even if one disagrees with certain matters of tone and emphasis, remains the standard work. It has an excellent bibliography.

Paul Addison, *The Road to 1945: British Politics in the Second World War* (1975), though more purely concerned with politics, is a valuable corrective. It also contains an up-to-date bibliography. There is a very down-to-earth, no-nonsense chapter in Henry Pelling, *Britain and the Second World War* (1970).

For a fuller development of my own views you could look at the relevant chapters in *Britain in the Century of Total War* (1968) and *War and Social Change in the Twentieth Century* (1974), and also at my 'People's War and Top People's Peace?' in *Crisis and Controversy: Essays in honour of A. J. P. Taylor* (1976). Paul Addison also has a valuable contribution to this book.

Excellent accounts of the domestic front without any great pretence at analysis are to be found in: Norman Longmate, *How we lived then* (1971); Leonard Moseley, *Backs to the Wall* (1971); and Susan Briggs, *Keep Smiling Through* (1975). Norman Longmate has also written on *The Real Dad's Army: the Story of the Home Guard* (1974), and on *The GIs: The Americans in Britain 1942–1945* (1975).

Both for giving the wider perspective, and for a marvellously succinct chapter on the Second World War, A. J. P. Taylor, *English History 1914–1945* (1965), is indispensable.

The really serious student will have to bury himself in the many volumes of the Civil Series of the official *History of the Second World War*, some of which are actually quite readable.

Among the less-familiar topics, scientific developments can be studied in Margaret Gowing, *Britain and Atomic Energy* (1964); Hilary and Stephen Rose, *Science and Society* (1969); and Guy Hartcup, *The Challenge of War* (1970). Useful recent books relevant to war and urban development are J. B. Cullingworth, *Environmental Planning*, vol. 1, *Reconstruction and Land Use Planning* (1975); K. Richardson, *Twentieth Century Coventry* (1972); and A. Sutcliffe and R. Smith, *Birmingham 1939–1970* (1974).

In the realm of communications and propaganda, Asa Briggs, *The War of Words* (1970), vol. III of his monumental *History of Broadcasting in Great Britain*, is a classic. Ian Maclaine is working on a history of the Ministry of Information and Nicholas Pronay will shortly publish a study of Mass Communications.

The most recent general survey of social policy is Derek Fraser, *The Evolution of the Welfare State* (1973); it puts less emphasis on the Second World War than does Maurice Bruce, *The Coming of the Welfare State* (1961); José Harris's careful essay, 'Social Planning in War-time: some aspects of the Beveridge Report', in J. M. Winter ed., *War and Economic Development* (1975), pp. 239–56, was published after this book was completed. Her conclusions are substantially the same as mine.

The serious study of social history in the post-war period has scarcely begun yet. An older collection of sceptical essays (including 'We are the Masters Now' by Anthony Howard of the *New Statesman*) is Michael Sissons and Philip French (eds), *The Age of Austerity* (1963).

Two recent novels which are perceptive on evacuation and the experiences of conscientious objectors are, respectively, Jackie Gillot, *War Baby* (1970) and Edward Blishen, *A Cack-Handed War* (1972). For the narrow segment of society they deal with, the Second World War novels of Evelyn Waugh are unsurpassable.

Photographic Acknowledgments

Department of Health and Social Security: 84; Imperial War Museum: 23, 32, 42, 50, 62, 74, 91, 94, 96, 97, 98, 99, 100, 116, 132, 135, 138, 139, 148, 152; Kent Messenger: *frontispiece*, 20, 27, 61, 75, 107, 144; Keystone Press Agency Ltd: 43, 48, 57, 83, 101, 105, 118, 140, 141, 142, 164, 165; Popperfoto: 1, 3, 5, 6, 7, 10, 11, 12, 13, 16, 17, 18, 19, 21, 22, 25, 26, 29, 30, 31, 33, 34, 35, 36, 37, 38, 39, 40, 41, 45, 46, 47, 49, 51, 52, 53, 54, 55, 56, 58, 59, 60, 63, 64, 65, 66, 67, 68, 69, 70, 71, 72, 73, 76, 77, 78, 79, 80, 81, 82, 85, 86, 87, 88, 89, 90, 93, 102, 103, 104, 106, 108, 109, 111, 112, 113, 114, 115, 117, 119, 120, 121, 122, 124, 125, 126, 127, 128, 130, 131, 133, 134, 136, 137, 143, 145, 146, 147, 149, 151, 153, 154, 155, 156, 157, 158, 159, 160, 161, 162, 163; Radio Times Hulton Picture Library: 8, 15, 92, 129, 166; John Topham Picture Library: 2, 4, 9, 14, 24, 28, 44, 95, 110, 123, 150.

Index